PAINTING THE NUDE

Art-in-Practice Series

Project Director: Edward A. Hamilton
Photographer: Burk Uzzle

OTHER BOOKS
Painting with Oils by Warren Brandt
Painting with Watercolor by Mario Cooper

PAINTING THE NUDE

GLENN HAMM

Art-in-Practice Series General Editor: Jerry G. Bowles

VNR VAN NOSTRAND REINHOLD COMPANY
New York Cincinnati London Toronto Melbourne

Van Nostrand Reinhold Company Regional Offices:
New York Cincinnati Chicago Millbrae Dallas

Van Nostrand Reinhold Company Foreign Offices:
London Toronto Melbourne

Published by Van Nostrand Reinhold Company
450 West 33rd Street, New York, N.Y. 10001

Published simultaneously in Canada by
Van Nostrand Reinhold Company Ltd.

16 15 14 13 12 11 10 9 8 7 6 5 4 3 2 1

CONTENTS

PREFACE

The ART-IN-PRACTICE SERIES introduces a staff-oriented approach to the design and editing of art instruction books. For each book in the Series, a well-known creative artist and acknowledged experts in the fields of book design, professional writing, and photography have combined their talents in order to render the most effective and stimulating learning experience possible through the printed page. Integrating print and pictures for a unified graphic design; capturing in writing the distinctive atmosphere surrounding the artist, as well as his techniques and instruction; visually documenting the artist at work and his step-by-step processes through dynamic photographs—these are the important visual-editorial concepts of the ART-IN-PRACTICE SERIES.

In *Painting the Nude* Glenn Hamm has condensed a great deal of information on all aspects of painting the figure. He has outlined and illustrated such topics as working with the model; the role of photography and lighting; and, particularly, the countless techniques and media with which he is acquainted, along with new procedures that he as an artist has discovered.

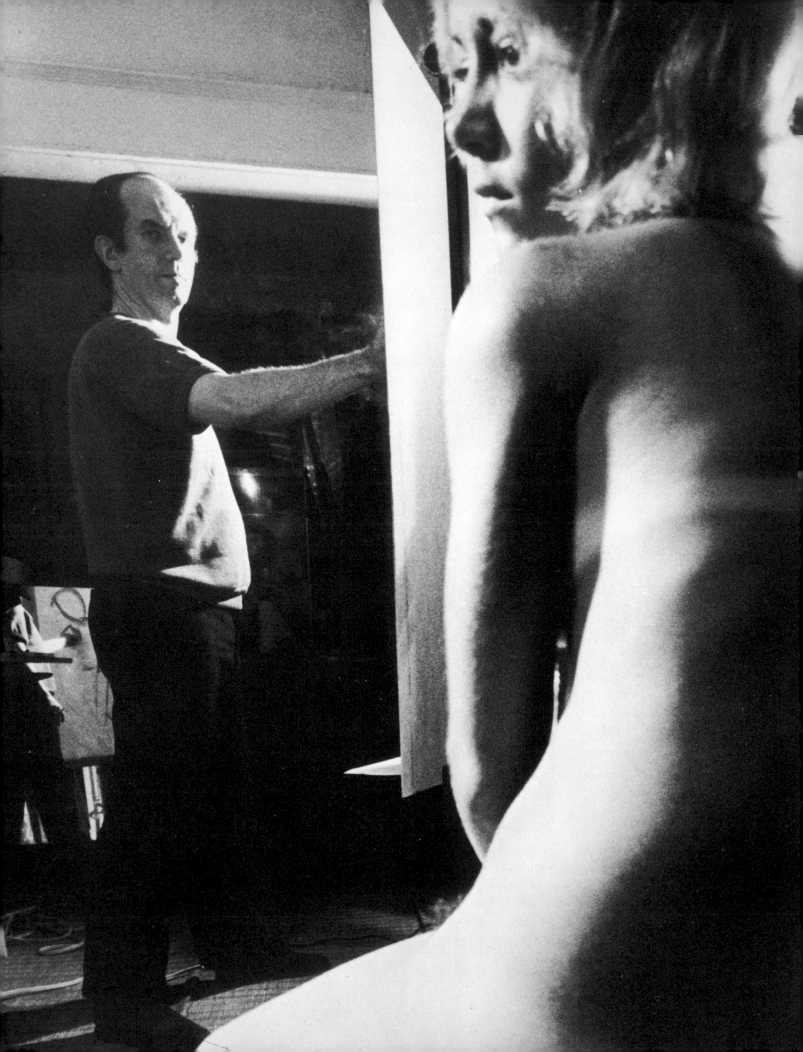

1 | SOME THOUGHTS ON ART

Art has been one of the most consistently important facets of my life since the day I decided to draw cartoon strips for my high school newspaper. Milton Caniff, of "Steve Canyon" fame, was a schoolmate of my father at Stivers High School in Dayton and so he was my natural hero. My uncle Carl and his son both either owned or managed commercial art studios in Dayton; my uncle Jack painted in oils and intended to be a fine artist during his younger days, and I still have my father's book of poetry and wood blocks that he printed himself when he was eighteen. He was also editor of the *Recensio* at Miami University in his junior year and, somehow, looking at the faded photos and the wood blocks of campus scenes so long ago inspired in me more respect for him than his job as an executive in the electrical engineering department at Sunshine Biscuit Company—because, I suppose, it seemed more timeless than devising new ways to electrically bake foodstuffs.

We do not all have to be artists, but we should learn some road to enlightenment in order to see life as full of creative potential. And we should take time to do things well.

Now I realize that I was something of a snob because my father did engineering well, and the erector set that he used to make a scale model of a fig-cutting machine (with the addition of specially tooled parts) was certainly kinetic sculpture. It was just a little ahead of its time and he needed an agent.

Doing things well no longer seems to be a valid or at least a dependable criterion in the unbelievably complex marketing arena of the modern art world. In fact, it is often seen as a drawback, hinting at sterility and academicism.

And yet, there are artists who are known for the ultimate in hard-edge perfection of design or who put the most loving care into polishing simple metallic shapes. From the primitive to the ultra-sophisticated, the rough to the polished, the simple to the complex; from a highly detailed traditional landscape to a "happening" where the artist kills a chicken or paints a nude model blue and has her roll in a sheet to make a body print—anything goes. Or does it?

Prizes are awarded to some and denied to others. Some artists are able to sell their work and others are not. Some are invested with the power to issue decrees on beauty and significance. By whom are they ordained? Who makes sense, establishes criteria, selects, determines values, accepts, rejects, exalts or casts away the artist's intimate and fragile productions?

The forces of the art world are the patron, the public, the critic, the aesthetic philosopher, the agent, the juror, the museum official, the teacher, and, finally, the last judge, the historian. All of these people have a piece of the action. It is a wise artist who can face this mélange and continue to do just what he believes in. It has been said that a competent artist learns to paint what the public likes; a great artist makes the public like what he paints—although he may not see the results in his lifetime.

Where does the artist fit in all this?

The artist produces the work which, in the best of all possible circumstances, would

Find a unique quality that is somehow present in all models.

be enough. But, if he is a commercial artist, he must please his client. If he is a fine artist, he must arouse the interest of the public in his work. He is affected by the critic's response, and must somehow reconcile himself to the advice of his agent or gallery director. The juror gets him in or kicks him out of important shows. He can award him prizes or deny them. If the artist has done well and has won a lot of prizes, he may be asked to be a juror, thus doubling up on roles.

The museum director may add the artist's work to his collection, and thereby enhance the artist's venerability. The university professor may include him in lectures on contemporary art or use his style as a model for comparison in studio courses. Finally, the historian may color his place in history according to his own bias and thought processes. This assumes that the artist makes it that far.

The public is generally far down in the line of influence in art circles. It is expected to abide by the "superior" tastes of the critic, the juror, the museum director, the teacher, and to especially venerate those artists of earlier periods exalted by the historian. People may grumble and say that their daughter could do a better job, but often they are afraid to say they dislike something for fear they will reveal some fundamental lack of knowledge. Yet, it is from these ranks that the future historians and patrons come and it is their steady, honest reaction over a period of centuries that finally determines the real worth of a work of art in human terms as opposed to the transient dust storms of art fashion.

Obviously, the most crucial person in the life of an artist is the historian, who has, after all, the final say. His decision often does not come during the lifetime of the artist.

The composite historical inclusion or exclusion of a given artist in books on art history probably has the most lasting effect on the public. The historian has the most lofty view, sees things in their greatest perspective, and should have the most impersonal and impartial notion of the true significance and impact of an artist on the course of art history.

This is not always true, of course, and we often find the same color plates of the same paintings over and over again building a legend about a certain few geniuses rather than widening the scope of human understanding to encompass more and more artists and their personal approaches.

Too often, art is used as a weapon of cultural or social power and is politically motivated—a means rather than an end in itself. If the three main attributes of God are Wisdom, Power, and Love, the materialistic contingent of the art world might be described as valuing power first, then wisdom, then love, if the latter can fit in somewhere. It is true of any large organization. Actually, the artist should value love first, because he is thoroughly capable of it; wisdom second, because he should constantly strive for it; and let him ignore power, because it corrupts.

The greatest works of art are only reflections of a higher beauty and truth one should strive for in personal relationships. I deal with the human figure because I feel that I understand it and can use it as a symbol for much that I find meaningful in life. I do not always state this in the most noble terms because life does not always manifest itself nobly. I *do* try to state my honest reactions, and hopefully the reader will find these throughout the pages of this book.

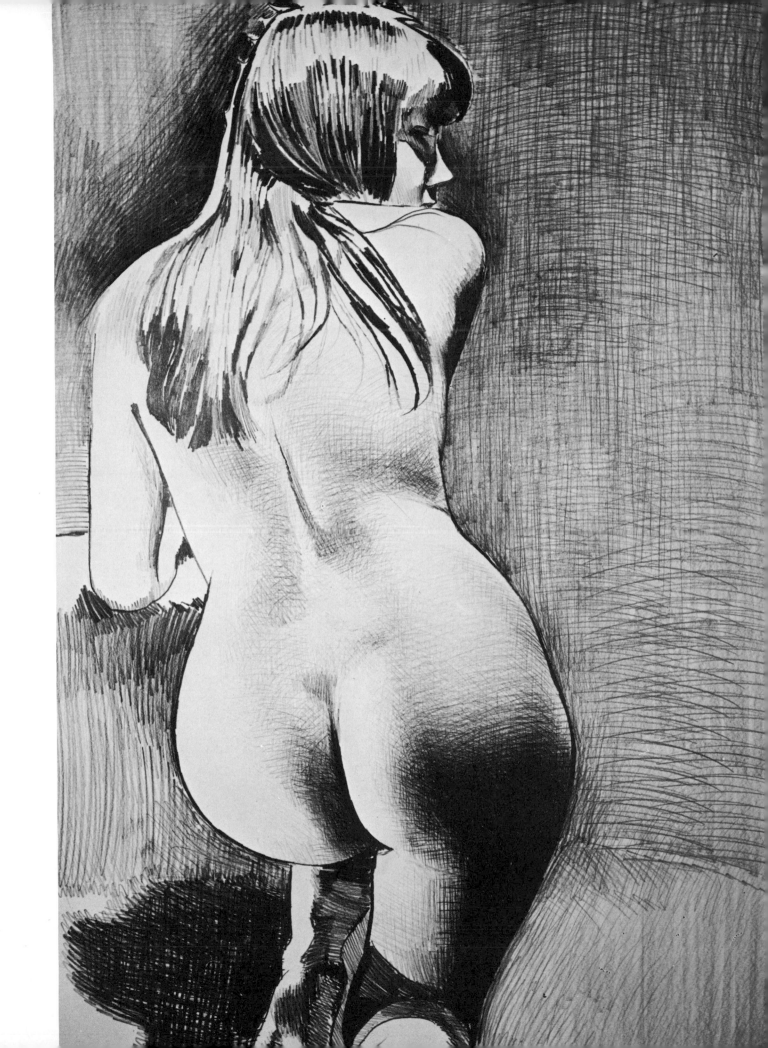

2 | WORKING WITH THE MODEL

One of the most difficult tasks for the figure painter is establishing a working relationship with the model. A good model usually has some creative experience in her background that enables her to empathize with the artist's needs, which are often expressed rather obscurely while he is drawing or painting.

Often intuitively, she adjusts a pose this way or that, turning the head the other way to balance the sideways thrust of a pose or adjusting an arm or leg which looks disconnected or awkward. Some models are also dancers and the discipline of the dance generally gives rise to very interesting and dramatic poses.

Often, it is wise to have a photographic session to capture fleeting poses and use the photographs for reference and free interpretation later on. Naturally, it is always better to work from life and a quick contour or gesture drawing often suffices to suggest the pose. However, many artists do not want a great deal of drama, since they feel that it looks artificial. They prefer a *genre* or "slice of life" approach—the model as she would ordinarily stand or sit in the home, for example. At any rate, the more natural poses are easier on the model, while a true action pose is almost impossible to hold after three to five minutes.

Although the artist has a tendency to be rather indifferent to the model, preferring to concentrate on his craft and the inner workings of his imagination, he should realize that the model is indeed a human being and responds favorably to praise and interest. It takes little effort to say that a certain pose is particularly effective or striking, or that he feels she is skillful, and finds that her efforts are beneficial to his work. If the model feels appreciated and is paid what she asks, the posing session is usually free of the scarcely veiled indifference and vague sluggishness that may otherwise intrude. Still, there are models with very abrasive personalities who are nonetheless visually effective.

Some artists ask the model to wander about aimlessly, standing, sitting, and so on, and then stop her suddenly when they see a pose they like. Often, the best possibilities occur between poses, when the model is more relaxed. However, in the beginning of a session, certain more specific instructions are usually helpful. If no initial comments are given her, the model may strike a couple of poses and then, on meeting the slightest degree of disapproval or indecision on the part of the artist, may look rather confused and say, "You'll have to tell me what you want"—which is rather difficult when you consider it: putting an imaginary pose into words.

A large mirror is always helpful, but not always available. With this simple device, the model is able to see what the pose looks like and also how the light disposes itself on her anatomy. Lacking this, the artist may choose from several other approaches: he may describe the pose he wants visually—for instance describing some of the main pose types discussed in the next chapter; or he may attempt to cause the pose to happen by mechanical or emotional suggestions. A list of some of these suggestions is shown in the chart on page 29.

In a three-hour session in which the model strikes a multitude of poses, one often notices three phases: awkward reticence at the beginning, playful experimentation, and tired resignation. These attitudes generally influence the character of the pose and the

Try to establish some interrelationship between two poses.

resulting artwork. An understanding of these influences can help the artist to either emphasize the different shades of emotion, or to resist them when he sees them coming. For example, in one session the model started by saying, "I don't know what kind of pose you want." Later, in a reclining pose, she said, "Those lights are too hot—how much longer do I have to hold this pose?" At this point, the muse had obviously gone, but genre poses were still possible.

Because of society's bewildering attitudes toward the unclothed body, some discussion of the visual concepts of modesty and eroticism is in order. The public will be disappointed to learn that in general the overwhelming preponderance of artist-model relationships mainly involve very hard work. It's hard to pose and hard to paint. Basically, it is also difficult to study or to teach, when these are embarked upon in a spirit of energetic concentration. But the effort is well worth it. There is no casual self-indulgence in the roles of artist and model. There is instead a craft, a calling, and an art. It is said that the amateur paints for the *fun* of it all; well, the professional paints for the *misery* of it all.

In terms of the artist's *use* of the pose, modesty, as a concept that is visually exploitable, is often affected by what *is* or *is not* shown. While showing the nude body in a work of art from almost any angle should be acceptable in an intelligent and more-or-less mature society, featuring *parts* that are normally clothed is often seen as rather unnatural and an artificial bid for sensationalism. Others will say that this development is a product of our times—therefore honest, and even healthier than other styles hearkening back to the classic past.

The figleaf had a tendency to attract attention rather than dissipate it, but it served its purpose in an age when anything shown had to be rendered in flawless detail. A European firm, specializing in sculptural reproductions a few decades ago, was supposed to have had three styles of nude figures: those with the figleaf for England; those without for most of Europe; and with a removable one for America. This story may be apocryphal, but it at least correctly indicates that social mores have quite a bit to do with the finished work of art.

The partially clothed figure tends to emphasize nudeness, and turn it into nakedness. This can be seen in much contemporary art, where although nakedness has its appeal, the spectator is often left with a vague embarrassment and a feeling of frivolousness not usually associated with significant art.

It is wise to allow the model to take at least partial breaks when the pose becomes tiresome, even if these occur at five-minute intervals.

Working with more than one model can be aesthetically fruitful, but the situation is more complex. Both personalities must be taken into account; the instructions are more difficult to verbalize; and the models tend to be distracted by each other. Best results occur when the models are friends, or (in the case of a male and female model) husband and wife, since there is a natural timidity about body contact with a stranger and this timidity will tend to produce two separate poses and a general awkwardness.

A sensitive model has the same need for creative meditation as the artist.

At the beginning of a session the artist must show the model the depth of his interest and expectations and by his manner and his gestures, perhaps even more than the words he chooses, transform her into an extension of his thoughts as well as an inspiration for them. An aesthetic union occurs—beautiful and rewarding. The artist and the model achieve fulfillment when each of their natural capacities are being utilized—the capacity to be and the capacity to do. While the artist responds kinesthetically to the model's gracefulness or power, the model empathizes with the artist's creative reactions and feels that she's accomplishing something of lasting value through his efforts.

In these photographs, an effective general pose is shown; however, because of the lighting and the viewpoint from the easel, I ask that the head and arms be twisted in another direction for a greater sense of total movement. Although precise and specific directions are sometimes necessary, they tend to confuse the model and, if indulged in to excess, even hinder her natural habits of movement.

At right. Drapery, backdrops, mirrors, and other unusual or inspirational effects can inspire both the artist and the model and result either in more creative poses or an environment more conducive to creative design effects in the painting itself.

Facing page. Every care should be taken to insure that the model feels that she is participating in something rather than simply being "looked at." Giving her a concept to experiment with helps to relieve self-consciousness, for nothing is more static than a person with nothing in particular to do.

Below. The model relates to environmental effects in ways that would be almost impossible to "fake" later. When there is a large mirror in the studio, the model should be encouraged to "paint herself" with the lights by turning or bending this way or that.

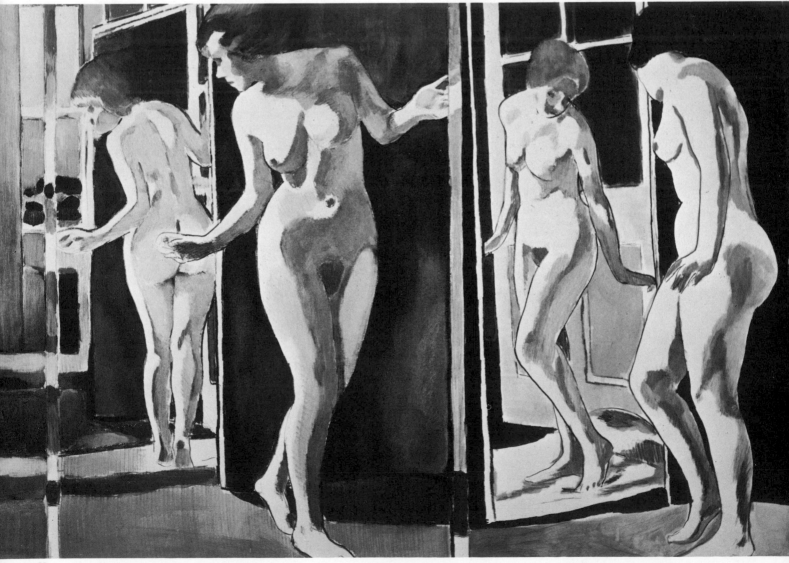

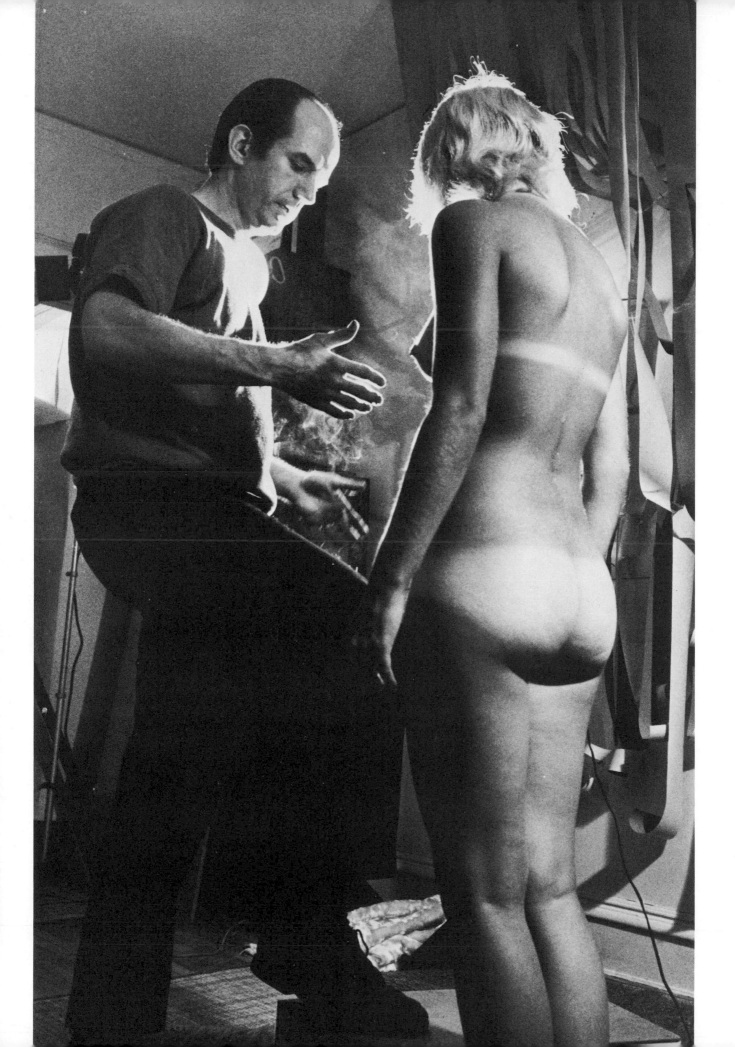

3 | MAJOR POSING CATEGORIES

Since the artist is often called upon to suggest a pose to the model, and must certainly approve of a pose before transforming it into a work of art, he should have some knowledge of the major posing categories. A convenient list might be: 1. Standing; 2. leaning; 3. kneeling-squatting; 4. seated; 5. reclining; 6. suspended; and 7. moving and purposeful action poses. Each category calls forth different emotions, different symbolism, and different problems in rendering or design.

In THE STANDING POSE, a study in balance, the center of gravity should be under the pit of the neck. Some of the more interesting poses in this category are achieved when the head, chest, and hips are tending in different directions. This includes any direction within the three areas of roll, pitch, and yaw. An interesting tension is also created when one part of the body gets out of balance and another part corrects this balance.

Standing poses that involve twisting and turning create still more emotion and rhythm.

One of the difficulties with standing poses is that they tend to be compositionally long and thin, especially if you want to include the entire figure on the canvas. There seems to be a general sameness about all standing poses in this regard, but the problem can be circumvented at times by showing only part of the figure; altering its silhouette with unusual light effects; or interesting involvement with the background and/or other figures. At any rate, something has to be done with all that "leftover" space. In the seated or reclining pose, because the figure is more or less wrapped up in itself, forming an oval or rectangular form, there is not much empty space left. The leftover space in the standing pose can also be utilized by having the figure bend over, extend the arms or legs, or hold some piece of costume or accessory.

THE LEANING POSE is automatically more unified than a standing pose because the figure needs the environment, or another figure, to keep from toppling over. This shared-weight relationship can be emphasized by having part of the object leaned upon overlap part of the figure, or by having the figure cast shadows on the supporting structure (such shadows being a distorted silhouette of the model herself and therefore in harmony with her form, although a part of the background).

The leaning figure is symbolically weaker than the standing one, but more informal and more flexible. Two figures may lean against each other, establishing complex crossbalancing to the point where they may appear to be performing acrobatics.

THE KNEELING POSE is more compact and usually affords a great number of opportunities to overlap parts of the figure. Since it is compact, the kneeling or squatting pose may take up so much of the pictorial space that there is really no room left for a background without crowding the composition.

Symbolically, the kneeling pose is perhaps the most descriptive of all the main pose types, often representing submission or obedience, and usually more fitting with the female figure (as in Oriental calligraphy, where the character for the male is standing and the female is kneeling). I hasten to add that this has nothing to do with my feelings about the relative rights of men and women in current society, but represents symbolic opposites in the primordial sense.

THE SEATED POSE is also very compact and relates strongly to the environment.

Many good poses can create the illusion of motion.

The model usually takes on a contemplative appearance. A great deal of the hips and legs are usually obscured, at least with respect to the lower contours, which tends to emphasize the head, chest, and arms. Since this pose is easier for the model to hold than many of the other types, greater detail is possible when rendering from life.

THE RECLINING POSE is basically a problem of understanding the "floor plan"—as in architecture, this is the exact area of the base plane occupied by the model. It is seldom a question of balance, as in standing poses, and therefore a host of utterly free and expressive movements are possible, any one of which can be held for an indefinite period of time. If the artist adopts a viewpoint almost directly above the model, he avoids much of the problem of foreshortening and achieves poses that may occasionally be turned up vertically to give the illusion of floating, flying, or other moving figures in a gravity-free situation. The model will often look radically different in a reclining pose, since gravity does cause the features, or portions of the anatomy, to sag.

Another way of analyzing reclining poses is to think of the model as an island in the ocean, with inlets, beaches, foothills, and mountains. This takes care not only of the "floor plan" but also the various elevations and angles of departure from the base plane. This is especially true when the figure is reclining flat on her back or on her stomach.

In order to establish a firm relationship between the figure and the base plane, cast shadows are extremely important. I find two types work in most situations. The first is the wider type of cast shadow, being a distorted silhouette of the contour of the figure itself, darker near the "terminator" or edge between the light and dark, with an inner reflected light. These cast shadows are sharper than the form shadows on the figure and represent a wedding of figure contour and surface conditions of the plane on which the shadow is cast, together with a third factor, the angle of the light source.

A second type of cast shadow could be called the "sliver" shadow, occurring between forms pressing against each other. The narrower it is, the harder the two forms seem to be pushing against each other. This phenomenon works throughout the body and should be mastered by any artist interested in the rendering of masses and their interrelationships.

THE SUSPENDED, OR FLOATING, POSE carries the dreamlike quality a step further, into the feeling of transcendence or metamorphosis. The figure seems to be going through a psychic transformation, or becomes the embodiment of a spirit. Spectators tend to find such poses unsettling, especially if there is no base plane or horizon line to relate to.

THE MOVING, OR ACTION, POSE should usually lean toward the aesthetically "impractical" rather than the purposeful—in which a figure relates to some useful work activity. This is certainly not a universal rule, however; it presupposes a desire for mystery and ambiguity. On page 29, I have made a list of suggested action archetypes.

A simple maneuver such as turning the torso brings a pose to life.

Often what seems to be a relatively simple pose can be very hard for the model to hold for any length of time. Here the model is partially standing, yet also in a sense kneeling backwards against her clasped hands. Soon her neck begins to stiffen and her natural instinct is to bring her head back up. As the minutes go by, the arch in her back begins to flatten out, and the delicate and supple counterbalancing becomes more prosaic. Her arms drop. The artist continues to draw the unchanged parts of the body until he reaches a point where he feels he must suggest that she take a break or try to inspire her to recreate the unique appeal the pose had at the start. The relationship between media and difficulty of pose is especially relevant. When the artist combines the slowest of media with the most demanding of poses, problems naturally crop up. Therefore, some form of shorthand or "plan now—finish later" strategy is imperative. Hard and soft edges of cast shadows can be indicated quickly and often developed while the model is resting or even long after she has left. Don't wait to introduce environmental surroundings into the composition until work on the figure has crystallized into its finished form, for the best time to inject fantasy or to invent design effects is while facing the unquestionable reality of the figure itself and developing them together produces a sought-after unity.

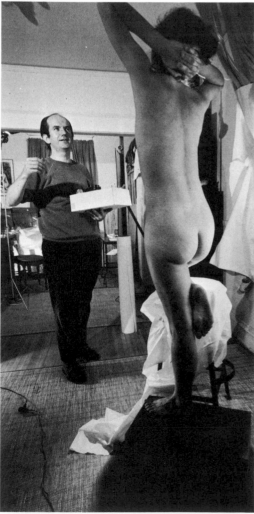

SOME MECHANICAL AND EMOTIONAL SUGGESTIONS FOR POSES

Put your weight on one leg and slouch.

Start out with the weight on both legs and both arms to the side. Keep your head forward. Shift the weight to the right leg and bend the left. Twist in the direction of the right leg. Raise the arms slowly, unevenly, but keep them pressed to the body. Keep twisting the body to the right. Begin to twist only the chest to the left until there is a definite separation of direction. Then, keeping every part as it is, twist the head back to the right and down. After this, still keeping the weight on the right leg and everything else as it is, slowly slide the left leg backwards as far as it will go and establish a general equilibrium.

Lie on your back and, with one hand, touch one ankle. (This tends to draw the body up into a series of curves and tensions.) Then, bring your head to the side, or as far back as it will go. Beginning with this pose, roll over to one side or another.

Imagine that you are ushering in the wind.

You are warding off a large flying creature.

You are beckoning, or calling, or opening your arms to receive someone or something.

The life is slowly ebbing from your body and you are about to collapse.

ACTION ARCHETYPES

One figure restraining the other.

A figure trying to break chains, ropes, other restraints—even invisible ones.

A figure trying to rise but unable to.

Lifting objects, or another figure.

Several figures holding each other up.

Pushing an object or another figure.

A figure viewing herself in a mirror or body of water.

Figures that are struggling, fighting, racing, or engaged in games or sports.

Figures moving in water, swimming, floating, diving.

Rolling or sliding figures.

Figures that are dancing or performing ritualistic motions.

Figures that chastize, stone, strike, or kill other figures.

One or more figures hiding.

Confronting a barrier or a restraining group of figures.

Facing page. In the woods or other rugged terrain, a standing or leaning pose is generally more acceptable to the model unless some covering is placed on the undergrowth. With the leaning pose, you effect a harmony between the figure and the tree that gives off almost a friendly aura and you also emphasize the textural differences between the bark and the model's skin.

This figure and pose are woven into the environment through an interlacing of cast shadows and open-and-closed areas. Balance is often achieved by a combination of the outer contours and the disposition of lights and shadows within the figure.

Above. In a forward-leaning pose, which would be quite simple and straightforward in profile, overlapping of forms or form and shadow is necessary to create the backward thrust of the figure in foreshortening. Such a pose seems very confusing and incorrect in pure silhouette, but the addition of staccato background elements keeps the figure from being read as a silhouette.

At right. In what is essentially the same pose, in profile and with the model leaning on the stool in this case, the problems of foreshortening are almost entirely absent. The Egyptians noticed the tendency of parts of the body to appear in their clearest archetype when viewed from a particular angle.

When the figure is seen from below, it takes on a heroic aspect, since the legs and hips are larger by comparison and the head slightly smaller. This generally produces strong overlapping of forms, and we see shadows underneath anatomical details which might go unnoticed at eye level. The artist is often presented with unique problems in this situation, for he's not used to seeing the lower plane of the eyebrow, nose, cheekbone, and other features. The use of the terminator, or accented dark immediately preceding the light area, is almost mandatory in indicating the lower plane of the hips pressing against the stool and yet avoiding excessive sharpness in the separation of the upper and lower forms.

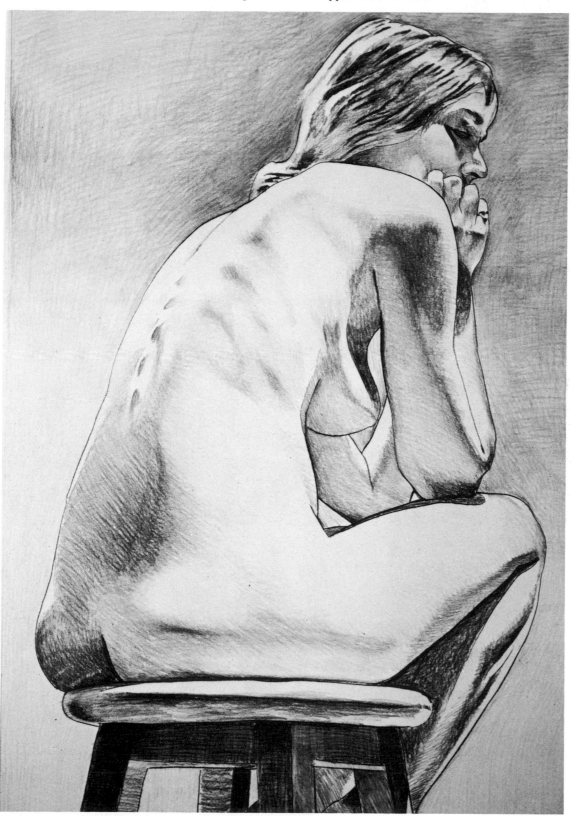

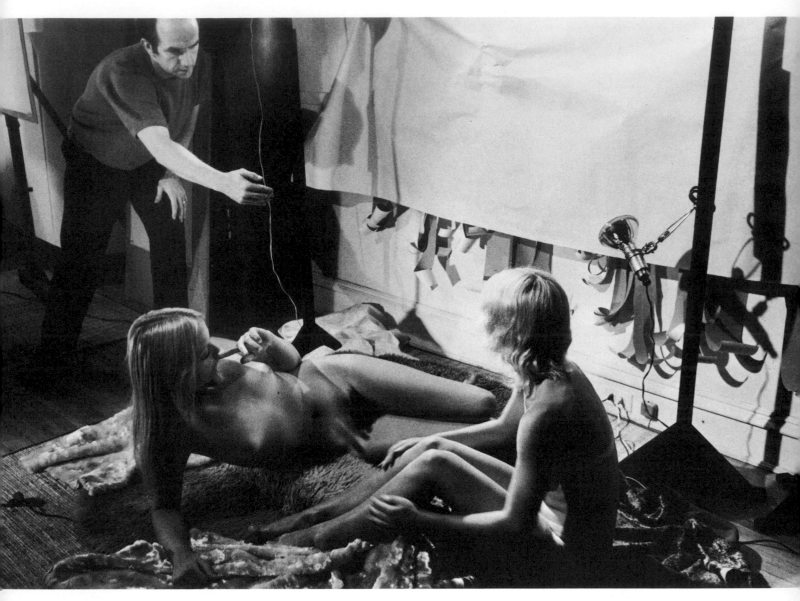

Posing problems are compounded when two models are used, but possibilities for overlapping of forms creating spatial effects, contrasts in mood, and unusual positive-negative juxtapositions multiply as well. At times it helps to think of the two models as a single creature with four legs, four arms, and two heads in order to achieve a flow of common intent throughout; however, on other occasions the figures are made to contrast in position and mood. In both cases, when two individuals interact in harmony or discord, you are dealing with more complex symbolism.

Facing page. After the model session, the artist gradually brings his drawing or painting into an archetypal world of his own personal ideals of beauty or design. He may emphasize or alter things to the point where they do not coincide with the situation at a later sitting, even if the model manages to adopt the identical pose. This phenomenon is also true when referring intermittently to a photographic reference. Although he may find certain new clues or nuances that he may want to add to his composition, it is seldom wise for him to change his aesthetic distillation to fit the reality of the model. Thus, protracted figure paintings represent more of a problem than those finished *alla prima*, but artists can profit from a second exposure to reality if the additions they make serve to mature the product of the imagination rather than to change it.

4 | IN THE STUDIO—
LIGHT AND EQUIPMENT

When the artist tries to arrange various light effects in his studio, he soon finds that in order to achieve chiaroscuro effects (the exaggerated groupings of tones into strong light and dark opposition), he needs small light sources that are capable of highlighting parts of the anatomy without producing so much light that they overlap and create a general flat diffusion. The flat-shape colorist, of course, would not be bothered by this nor would the professional photographer. It has been said that photographers hate shadows, while artists love them—at least artists interested in the effects of light on explicit forms.

One of the problems encountered in arranging for dramatic lighting is that the best light in which to see the model is often very poor light in which to work. It is hard to think of much color subtlety when the palette table and easel are lost in shadow.

Several choices are open at this point:

(a) For one, the artist can feature the light on the model and try to get used to the surrounding darkness. This is not as bad as it might seem, since the resulting color and value contrasts often tend to be more dramatic than when the normal room lights are turned on and add a feeling of mystery to the session.

(b) On the other hand, the artist may sacrifice some of the lighting on the model stand in order to have better light at the easel and then simply exaggerate the effects he sees as he begins the painting.

(c) It is also possible to have alternate sessions of looking at the model in strong light, followed by a period of painting under room lights while remembering the main light and shadow masses.

(d) A fourth possibility for consideration would be to capture the chiaroscuro effects via photography which has the added advantage of supplying a multitude of reference shots after the model is gone. I utilize all these approaches from time to time.

Lest all this seem too complicated, I hasten to assure the reader that artists today, as their ancestors did centuries ago, quite often grab a piece of paper and a stub of a pencil and simply draw their model lying on her couch or sitting on the edge of a bed in whatever light happens to be available.

What follows now may seem to many to be an unnecessarily long list, but, believe me, it could even be longer. These are things I have actually carried with me to a session with the model. Most of them fit into three suitcases of average to small size. (This list assumes that you may want to take some reference photographs and, thus, includes photographic equipment also.)

1. Drapery, for the model or background. Satin, cotton, some opaque and some translucent, enough for makeshift costumes and also enough to cover the model stand.
2. Still-life objects: flowers, silver globes, peacock feathers, stuffed elk, and dried rutabaga. In short, miscellaneous.
3. Hair clips, nets, and so on, for arranging hair styles.
4. Scarves, bandanas, jewelry, and brief costumes for semi-nude studies.
5. Rolls of paper for covering dirty floors, and to improve the reflective quality of the background.
6. Masking tape; scissors; knife; tacks, push pins; and staple gun and staples. All these

A few lightweight props can change the basic nature of a composition.

items I use to put up paper and cloth and to arrange the environment.

7. Books, photos, and samples of art work to show the model some of the poses and attitudes I prefer. These suggestions generally prove very inspiring to her, and it is a good idea to give her some prints of the resulting photographs, when you take any.

8. Makeup such as clown white, liner, gold makeup, and the like; cold cream, for makeup removal; absorbent cotton, Kleenex; paper towels. All these items are for special effects and are not always necessary.

9. Photographic lights—some photofloods and some spots. These are generally 150 to 300 watts, but most circuits won't take too many of them. The spots are more effective, because two photofloods can wash out the whole room in flat light.

10. Extension cords. You can never have too many, since they afford flexibility. In addition, "octopus outlets" permit many cords to be plugged into one wall socket.

11. Pliers and screwdrivers are always necessary to tighten up pesky lights that loosen and slump, pointing straight at the floor in the middle of a stupendous pose. And when all else fails, I have on hand "C" clamps to hold things up.

12. Small fur rugs soften the wooden model stand and make the model feel more sensuous. Pillows and similar props permit variety in reclining poses.

13. A very lightweight, full-length mirror. I don't always take this, but the effect is noticeable when I do. The model's interest increases when she can see her own body and your comments about light make more sense.

Then, the rest of the equipment consists of:

 A. A single-lens 35mm. camera.

 B. An identical 35mm. camera with strobe unit attached. This time-saving equipment precludes having to change the setting from flash to room lighting.

 C. A 2¼" square single-lens reflex camera.

 D. Lens cleaner; lens tissue; and a tripod.

 E. An exposure meter (although most of the recent 35mms. have through-the-lens meters).

 F. Filters: K2 Yellow improves contrast without distorting too much or cutting down on the exposure index to the point where you're forced to use the tripod all the time. Green and red filters are very dramatic, but often remove nuances of flesh tone.

 G. Accessory lenses as needed.

 H. Film, 35mm.; film, 120. Tri-X allows speed in dimly lit rooms, but Panatomic-X has less grain.

 I. A pencil or pen; a pad for logging exposure times or other information.

 J. A wristwatch for timing exposures, allowing breaks, and calculating how much the session is going to cost.

This chapter will deal with lighting that is at the command of the artist and photographer. When he leaves the studio and the world of electricity behind, the artist often finds himself in an entirely different situation, although a battery-powered flash unit may still give him some sense of security. He must make certain substitutions in his equipment list and procedures.

Spotlights and stands are cumbersome but especially useful to the chiaroscuro artist.

At left. Plain white bond paper, brown kraft paper, or rolls of various colored papers—all of which can be purchased inexpensively—can be formed into paper sculpture which catches the light in a more decisive way than soft drapery. The paper can be slit and fringed, crumpled, scored, and folded to create massive abstract effects and, with the use of a raking light which plays on the forms at a very shallow angle, to bring out exaggerated light and shade.

Below. In an old studio or classroom, an entire surrealistic façade may be created in half an hour with the use of a staple gun. If the situation does not permit stapling directly into the wall, a light skeleton framework of 1″ x 2″ pine or furring strips can be constructed for this purpose and disassembled afterwards for future use. The general dreamlike quality of the background being reminiscent of a party, a dance, a stage setting, or simply disguising the cold reality of an otherwise featureless room, influences the model's approach to the session.

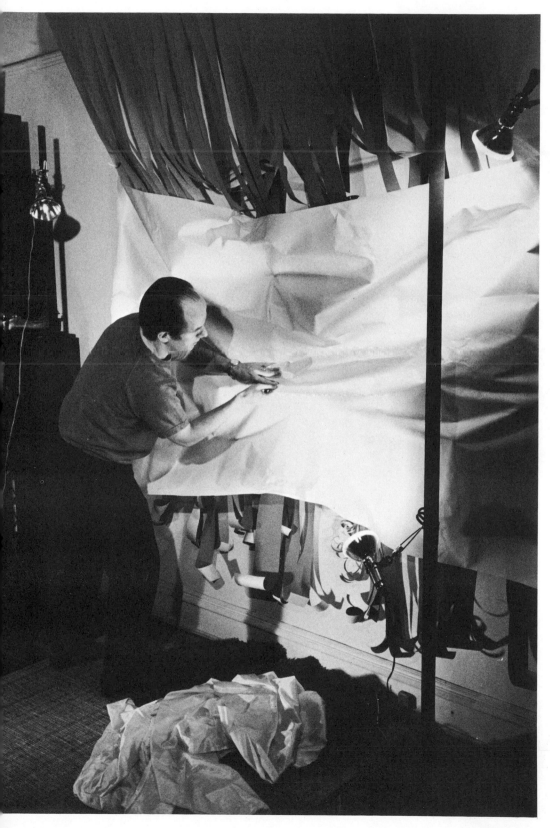

Notice the difference in the details on page 38 between the top and bottom photographs, which were taken with general, flat room lighting; the increased sculptural interest that begins to develop on this page; and the exaggerated, almost cavelike quality in the finished work on pages 142–43. Using pronounced forms keeps the artist constantly reminded of the possibilities of exaggeration for the sake of greater mass and form in the figure itself.

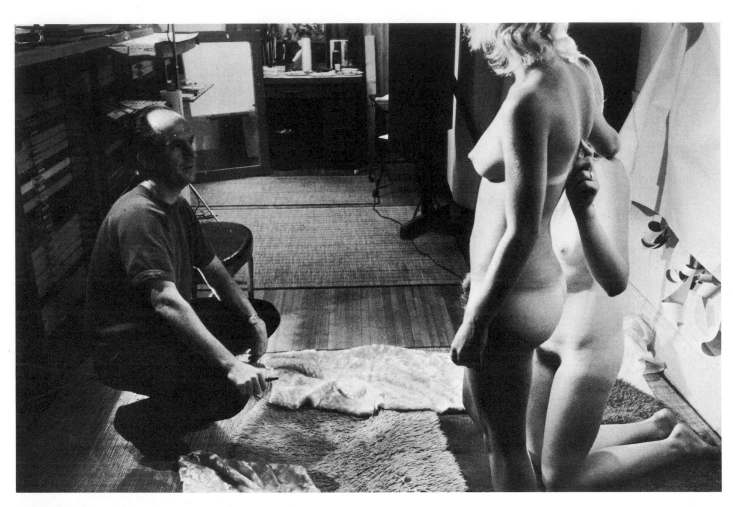

Above. The use of a great deal of paper also improves the reflective qualities of the environment as the light bounces off these surfaces and brightens up the internal parts of the shadows on the figures. It is often very effective to use a cool-color paper to produce dramatic bluish half-lights which are contrasted against the warm main lights as well as the general local color of the skin.

At left. An abundance of casual drapery and cushions on the floor can help create a more friendly and receptive environment for the models and keep them from feeling overwhelmed by equipment.

Facing page. A studio with a confined or narrow floor space seriously limits logistics, but this situation is encountered quite often, except in large classrooms. Therefore, it's a matter of achieving the greatest flexibility and maneuverability between four key points: the artist, the easel, the model(s), and the light(s).

Overleaf. By integrating several figures in the same painting or drawing and placing the figures in different perspectives, you can create a surrealistic effect and still maintain the integrity of the drawing itself.

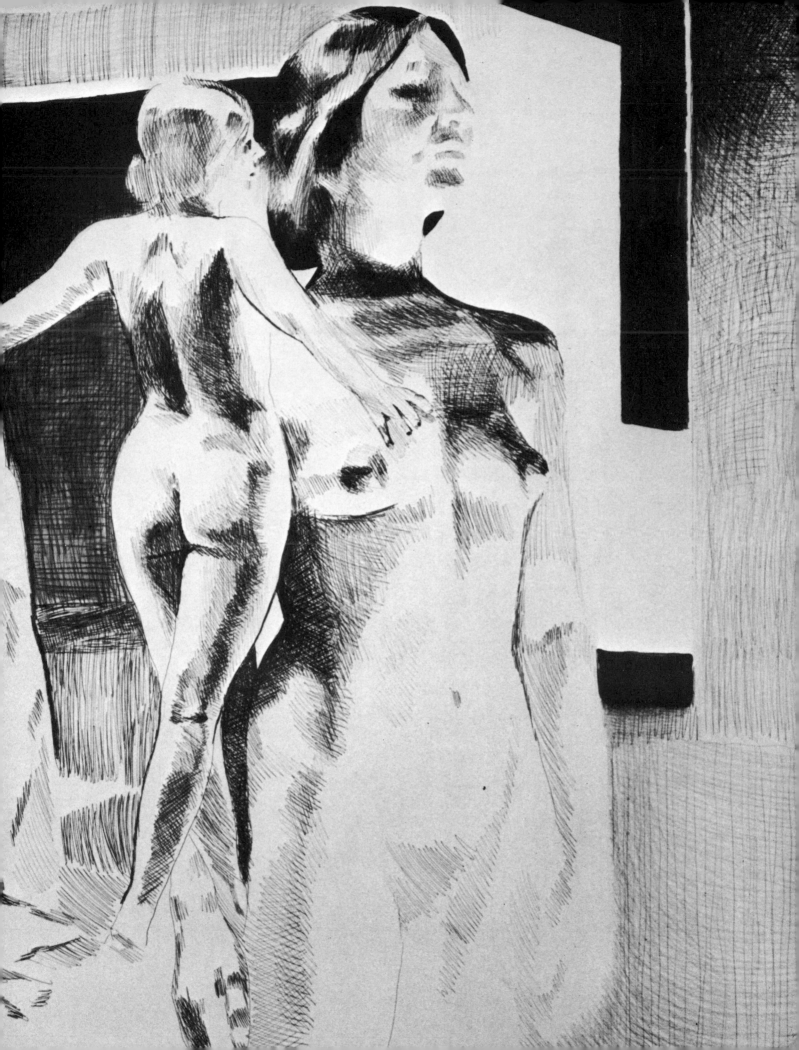

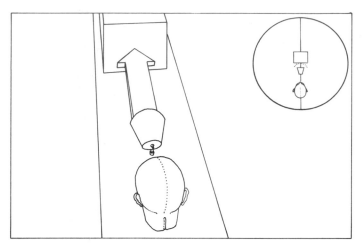

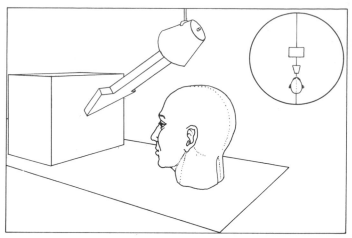

Flat lighting. The light source illuminates the model directly along the path of vision of the viewer. This kind of lighting is characteristic of flash and strobe-light photographs and represents the flattest, most documentary, and most common artificial light.

Flat lighting—from 45° angle above. Similar effects are produced here: the model often looks younger and more rhythmic in this light, but less character comes through. More palpable mass and shadows collect under the forms.

Flat lighting—from 45° angle below. This lighting schema is the exact opposite of the usual class relationship of model, viewer, and outdoor sunlight, and so the results can be rather weird and ghostly. Commonly used in stage lighting, it produces dramatic effects as well.

Three-quarter front lighting. The light creates more massive effects here, but since it is at level height it does not strongly feature either the under or upper planes, and since it is mainly frontal, there will be more light than shadow on the figure.

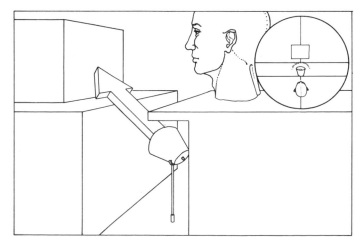

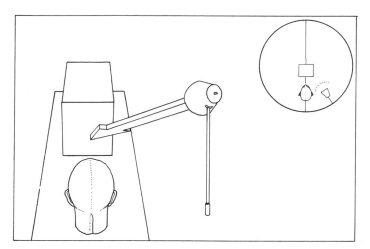

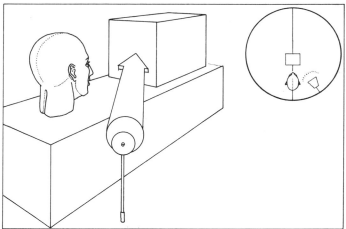

Three-quarter front lighting from above. Here the forms of the figure are not only lit slightly to one side, but the top planes catch the light as well. Strong planes are established under the shoulder blades, buttocks, elbows, and so on.

Three-quarter front lighting from below. Notice the dramatic quality of low lighting coupled with greater mass as the shadows widen out to the side. The figure must be standing or placed on a surface well above the floor plane to position the lights below.

90° side lighting. This scheme should produce the most evenly distributed set of light and dark shapes on the figure, in a design sense, and it is interesting to put the model in a crossfire of lights from both sides. However, the results may prove confusing, because of the mixture of light sources.

90° side lighting from above. The light here is clear, sharp, and unobstructed. The figure is aligned with the flow of light, which picks out only the high spots here and there as in raking light.

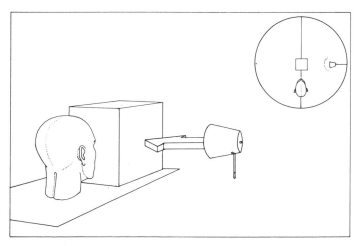

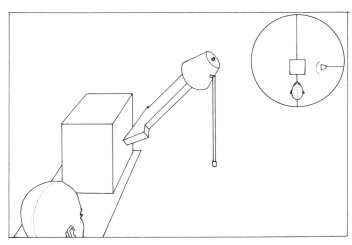

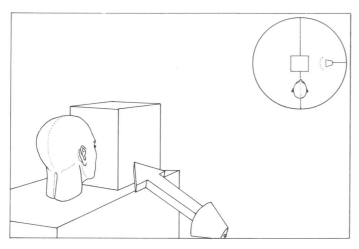

90° side lighting from below. You risk a greater degree of off-balance composition when all the major lights deposit themselves either to the lower right or lower left.

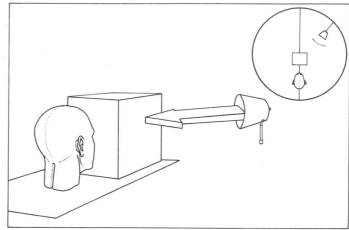

Three-quarter lighting from the back. The model has a tendency to move toward us and into the shadows with this light. We feel as if we are looking at the back of the picture instead of the front, where the light source must be.

Three-quarter back lighting from above. Shadow occupies the majority of the figure, as in a crescent moon, and the upper planes are lighted. Great clarity and sculptural reality are possible with this lighting.

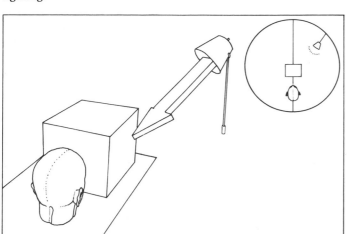

Three-quarter back lighting from below. Here again, the loftiness of the pose may be increased by virtue of the fact that we are looking up at the model and also because the light is shining upward.

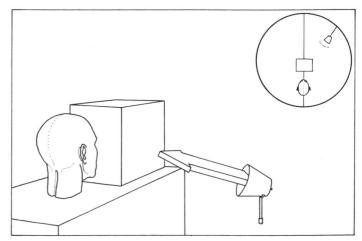

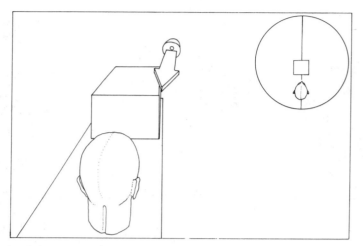 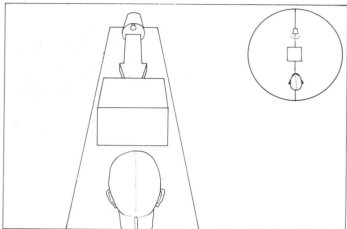

Raking light. This angle, which lights up the greatest detail possible, is used in studying the impasto work on oil paintings when determining authenticity. It is like early dawn or sunset light which picks out the most amazingly explicit forms and textures.

Rim lighting. The model is essentially reduced to a silhouette with gleaming edges in this light. You can scarcely achieve greater mystery with lighting unless you resort to the blank shadow silhouette. No major side shadows and no upper or lower planes are illuminated.

Top lighting. This is the most natural of lighting sources since we are accustomed to the shadow patterns caused by the sun. It tends to create flat slabs on horizontal figures or parts of the figure that are more or less horizontal.

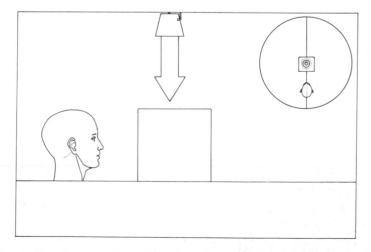

The lighting scheme here is a combination of 90° side lighting from the lower right, and 90° side lighting at level height from the left.

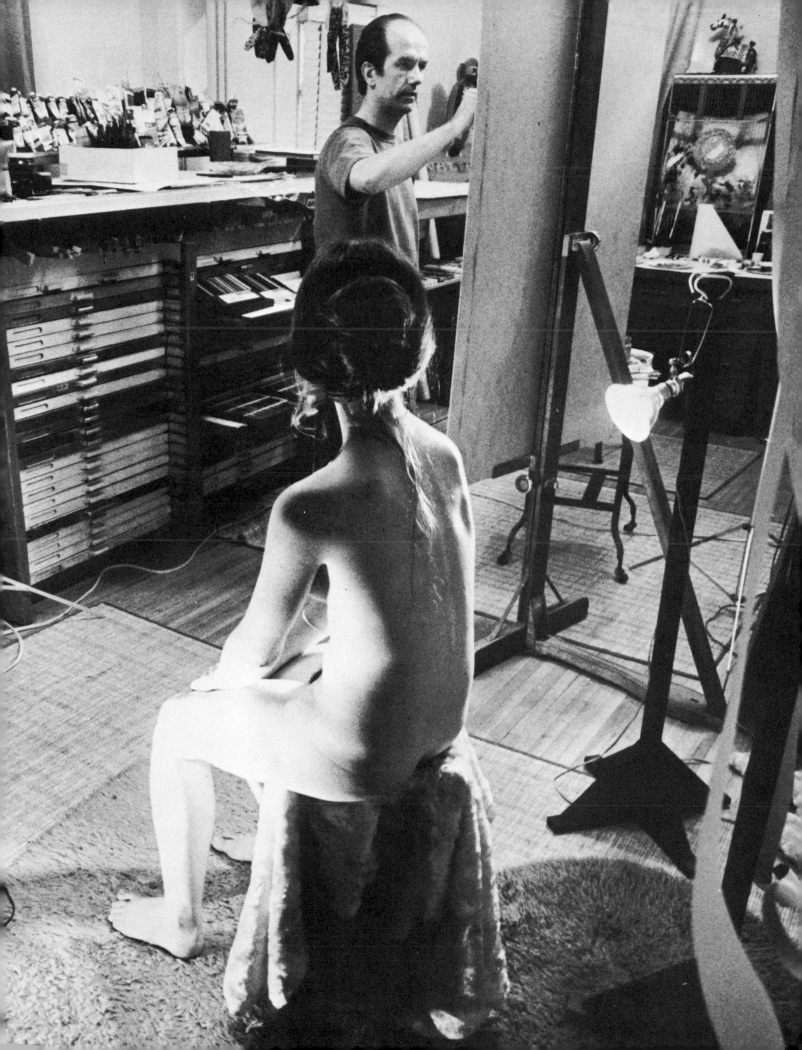

This demonstrates a three-quarter lighting source.

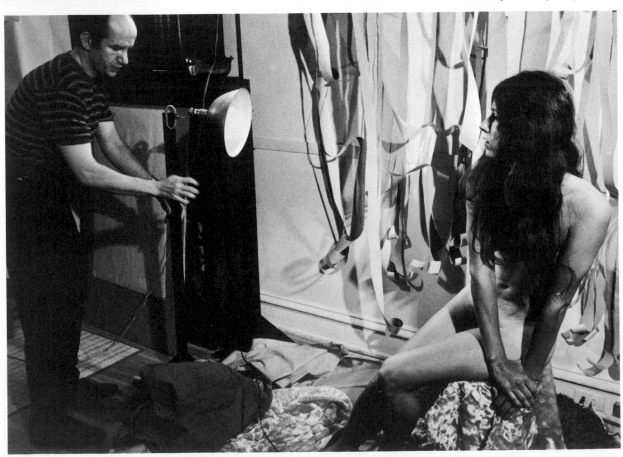

The model is surrounded by three-quarter front lighting from below and rim lighting from above and behind.

5 | OUTDOOR LIGHTING

Studio lighting is difficult, but nowhere as hard as searching for light effects out-of-doors. It is one thing to photograph a nude with a single-lens reflex camera as she gambols about among the breakers on a dazzling stretch of beach in the salty spray. It is quite another to set up an easel and attempt to mix oils without getting sand in them; to paint on a canvas without having it blown away down the beach; or to move the whole production twenty feet ashore to escape a sudden wave.

There are times when photography is almost essential if certain candid poses and effects obtained outdoors are to be recorded. However (and this is an important note), the photograph must always be the servant and not the master. When he uses his own photographic references in his studio, the artist must remember the spirit of the day and the moods and aspects of the light, of forms and space which the photograph can never record, and he must emphasize these warm human responses over and above the mechanical photographic guide—which is only a rather harsh souvenir of what was an actual living experience. *And*, he must have had a great deal of experience in working from the live model.

It is almost impossible to arrange for light effects to happen in the open—as on the beach or in the desert or by a swimming pool—and there is always a certain preoccupation with possible stray spectators who might be curious and disruptive. Nevertheless, the simple elegance of sunlight, whether in the raking light of early morning, or sunset, or the uncompromising intensity of the noonday sun, is perfect in its own way. It is more a question of waiting for the right things to happen than trying to make them happen.

The forest is often a more interesting situation for establishing light effects and composition, since the trees and vegetation present a great variety of possibilities for blocking the sunlight, and creating rays or bands of light with their corresponding shadows. Trees, bushes, rocks, and other objects may be used as natural props for the model to touch, hold, sit or recline on, lean against, and so on. They may also be utilized to block part of the figure and so change the normal contours.

In the forest, there is the feeling of quiet sanctuary. The figure and these surroundings suggest an intimacy and seclusion that we do not necessarily feel with a study of a sunlit nude alone in a forty-acre field of freshly mowed alfalfa. The latter gives off a sense of independence and vastness, whereas with the figure in the woods, the appeal is that of belongingness and secretiveness.

In addition to the mechanics of lighting in the studio and the discovery of opportune situations during outdoor sessions, there are a number of ways an artist may vary the lighting mentally, producing effects that were never really there.

TWO-DIMENSIONAL LIGHTING

The artist may seek to solidify his composition—especially if formed from reference material taken in different lighting situations—by selecting a "two-dimensional light source." That is to say, he will choose one corner of his pictorial surface as the light source—for example, the upper right-hand corner. This means that all elements in the composition will tend to be light on the right contour edge and also the top. Conversely, they will be dark

The artist tries to establish some order out of the myriad of ever-shifting patches of light in which everything is immersed.

at the lower edges and at the left. This process may be utilized along with naturalistic lighting, but when the two techniques conflict, a choice must be made. This is a wonderful way of lending a cameolike three-dimensionality to line drawings as well as adding the effect of "space pockets"—creating the illusion of digging behind contours of featured elements. I find this approach especially useful in the dry-marker monochromatic media, such as pencil and pen and ink.

LIGHTING AND FOCUSING FOR EMPHASIS

One may vary the intensity of light—its amount and placement—and the resulting effects on the forms in the composition. The principle here is that when light picks out strong contrast and profuse detail, the object is emphasized. When the reverse is true, when the light diminishes, contrast wanes and detail becomes blurred. This effect may also be achieved by the grouping of hues or high intensities in the desired areas.

It is also desirable, occasionally, to create light effects where they did not exist if they are needed to balance the composition.

ATMOSPHERIC OR AERIAL PERSPECTIVE

The more familiar linear perspective deals mainly with mass and space, whereas aerial perspective has to do with light and the persistence of selective reflected lights (hues) through greater and greater densities of atmosphere until they disappear into what may conveniently be called "infinity." We know that sunlight is made up of hues: red, orange, yellow, green, blue, indigo, and violet. Any surface receiving sunlight is receiving all of these colors. It selects one dominant wavelength to reflect and absorbs the others. Thus, a red paper is selectively reflecting red, and selectively absorbing orange, yellow, green and the rest of the colors. The further away we are from this red paper, the more layers of atmosphere (we could call it a blue-violet for the sake of convenience) are built up in front of it, imparting a blue-violet cast to the original red, which deepens until it merges with the prevailing blue-violet of the distant haze at the horizon. The artist may choose any *infinity color* and any *foreground color* in his compositions. If his canvas is painted red (representing infinite distance in this case) and an object nearest to us in this composition is blue, then he has the two prerequisites necessary for simple aerial perspective, namely a foreground color and an infinity color. To make a color recede in the red infinity distance, he simply mixes red with it on the palette—and, voila, it recedes. In this way the artist can vary his spatial effects via the light in his composition with the utmost precision, although with simple aerial perspective, the results are more like infrared heat recordings, in which all forms have intensely bright lights in the middle and diminish as they recede away from us. There are no sharp edges. These graduated effects occur within each rounded form, but individual forms themselves are picking up more and more "infinity-color saturation" (in this case, red) as they recede into the distance.

We shall discuss more complex aerial perspective and other ways of mentally altering a picture in Chapter 7.

Photography is especially appropriate in outdoor work, where often there is simply too much to be recorded in a small amount of time.

Below. The light effects are intimate, unique, and unpredictable. It is no longer a question just of sunlight, but light through countless "projectors"—small openings in the leaves which form natural, glassless lenses, like a pinhole camera or *camera obscura* that actually has focal points although the general diffusion muffles the effect.

Above. The verticality of the figure and trees, dappled and splashed by the vibrating islands of light, say something about our planet and the sun which illuminates it and gives it life. Suddenly it is the artist who seems out of place, an intrusion of intellect. . . . The figure is in a green cathedral . . . at home in a close and comforting natural structure to which it relates.

While trying to achieve the pose's best compass direction in relation to the sunlight, the artist and the model experiment with ways of conveying a natural languidness in order to enhance the feeling of belongingness emanating from the model and to have her appear to be nude rather than naked.

Outdoors, unforeseen problems arise which may either have a comical or irritating aspect, depending on your mood at the moment. The board is heavy, the tubes of paint spill in the water, you're thirsty, the previous painting has wrinkled the rest of your paper, the model sat on a muddy stone, the mosquitoes are out—your dedication is threatened by these ever-present reminders of our corporeal reality. A moment comes when the artist and the model both have the feeling that this situation is a little ridiculous, tiresome, and unproductive. However, with obstinacy, it is possible to get the work started, and soaring—at least for a half hour until some other minor emergency arises. Painting outdoors is physically hard work for all concerned and should not be attempted until the artist has had a fair amount of studio experience. Good habits of paint mixing and brush cleaning, and so on, become very important if any kind of subtlety is to be achieved in outdoor work, and you will appreciate paintings of woodland nudes much more after you have tried to paint them yourself.

In any type of outdoor landscape, when imaginative or narrative effects are added, or simply developed out of the existing situation by various additions, the use of pronounced light effect helps to make such compositions more than mere diagrams or cartoons. Notice the contribution of the light effects in the painting on the opposite page, how light establishes depth—pulling the figure forward out of the rather complicated background. The prismatic breakup of color also lends a unique quality to the light. Through it all, the gracefulness of the female figure is preserved.

Facing page, top. Take only what you'll really use, because you won't use much if you wear yourself out carrying it through the woods.

Facing page, left. A flat-shape style with a large brush and bold decisions is often the best way to capture the total light effect.

Facing page, right. When viewed through squinted, almost closed eyes, the model seems to partially disintegrate in the explosion of light.

If the painting is going well, the artist has the feeling that somehow he will preserve a sample of this moment in life that cannot be artificially produced. You can take home a box of leaves and stones, but this is the way to take home the moment.

6 | CREATING LIGHT AND SHADOW

In discussing the treatment of light, we might deal with the ways in which the artist (a) translates effects of light seen in nature into various media, each of which have certain tendencies and characteristics which make this translation either an easy or difficult thing to do, and (b) causes a metamorphosis in which light effects seen in clouds, water, land masses, and so on, are stated in terms of other identities, such as the human form.

The following might provide a helpful set of guidelines when using different materials to achieve effects of light:

Oils tend to be a rather heavy medium; some people call them a winter medium, preferring to use watercolors after the first warm spring day. I wouldn't stress such a strong demarcation, because, in the first place, oil painting can mean a variety of things, depending on the precise combination of media used:

Palette knife work with stiff impastos tends to produce a massive glowing quality, especially suited for effects of close value and high intensity.

Half-covering or translucent overlays of oils with a fair amount of media are admirably suited to capturing the opalescent or pearl-like quality of human flesh, especially the warm and cool contrasts of the Caucasian skin tones. We feel that we can see into the paint film, just as we can into translucent flesh.

Transparent *turpentine washes* are a great deal like frescoes, producing a fresh, fragile innocence of color which allows much of the white ground to show through.

Glazing a rather monochromatic underpainting with color, which pushes all the detail behind an overlying tone, then *heightening with light colors* to pull out form and brilliance, allows the artist to achieve tremendous substance and three-dimensional qualities. He may use this technique to produce very realistic figures under such precise and explicit lighting that each muscle is described in flawless detail, or he may elect to allow parts of the body to fade into a general haze.

As versatile as oils are, however, it is difficult to recapture the original freshness of the light effects once the color has been overlaid or reworked too often, destroying the reflective properties of the white ground.

Watercolors are a virtuoso medium capable of capturing fresh nuances of limpid color—impressions of light in clouds and water, and other ethereal effects. They are not as useful in achieving more deliberate academic renderings and allow very little reworking. The negative approach of leaving raw paper for the strongest lights is almost mandatory here, although it is often hard for the inexperienced artist to think in these terms. He must, for example, paint the light contour of a leg by putting dark background behind it. The light parts of the figure are not painted—they are surrounded by other colors. This effect can capture the dazzling qualities of sunlight, since the white watercolor paper reflects back most of the light it receives.

This reflective brilliance is true of all the waterbase materials, even the opaque media such as gouache, acrylics, and caseins, as well as egg tempera. The whites, which are generally important in creating light effects, are much more gleaming than in oil paints, which have a gray overcast by comparison. The opaque waterbase media are useful in achieving flat-plane interpretations of the model, where the figure is faceted like a diamond

Visual mixtures allow amazing control over the effects of light.

and each facet reflects a slightly different hue, value, or intensity in relation to the light source.

Pastels permit an amazing freedom in the use of color nuances; prismatic effects may be achieved wherein a flat color may have many other colors subtly introduced into it without seriously breaking down the integrity of the shape. For the purposes of this discussion of media in relation to the type of light they best describe, pastels produce an iridescence like that of a seashell. It is almost impossible to handle these luminous effects of trace colors or incidental flashes of will-o'-the-wisp ghostly blushes and pallors in, for instance, acrylics, which lay down a surface like a rubber raincoat in comparison. However, similar light effects *may* be achieved in acrylics and other media through the technique of scumbling, which is the use of dry brush application of almost dry color through a great amount of rubbing with the brush, usually a hog bristle (though a sable will produce a very delicate luminescence when scumbling on shiny surfaces).

The use of visual mixtures, whether in pen and ink, scratchboard, or etching and its companion techniques, allows an amazing control over the effects of light on form, since these networks of small dots, interrupted or continuous lines, may be woven over each other in different directions a countless number of times until a subtlety of tone is achieved in main and reflected light. Form and cast shadows, with their hard and soft edges, are easier to achieve through the slow logical buildup of visual mixtures than with continuous tone media.

I know artists who feel that to use any scientific approach to the lighting of the model is unnatural and eccentric. They believe one should take things as they come, look up briefly to see what fate has decreed on the model stand, and then start squeezing paint out on the palette. I have had students who objected to the use of spotlights because they occasionally glared in their eyes and seemed to prefer the familiar overhead fluorescent lights even though they gave the studio all the drama of the dentist's waiting room.

Choices are confusing at times and many artists with frail or transient interest would rather not know they exist. At least, they wish others would make their decisions for them. These people will find this chapter and the following ones on color disconcerting as an ever increasing spectrum of possibilities unfolds.

Dealing with light is a challenge that the artist ignores at his peril, since it is the quality, amount, angle, and treatment of light in various media that give all but truly nonobjective works of art their most striking impact. It has been said that a preoccupation with light is characteristic of the greatest eras in the visual arts.

The quality of light carries with it emotional and lyrical overtones. Compare the hard unobstructed light of the sun as it falls on the craters of the moon with the moody sfumato, or misty blending of the lower layers of a swampy forest on an autumn evening.

Notice the unique differences between soft form shadows and sharp cast shadows.

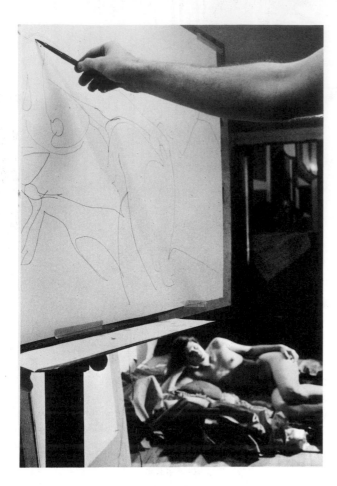

A translucent flat-plane or faceted approach to light and shadow seems to have more substance when preceded by a preliminary contour drawing. It is not a case of filling in the spaces but rather of flooding limpid shadows up against thin, decisive barriers. This middle tone—which can be left for reflected lights once the terminators of the shadows are deepened—may jump its barriers suppressing distant contours. The exact same tone may be used to accentuate foreground contours. Try to achieve as much solidity and cogent lighting with the most translucent tones for a pearl-like opalescence, for when the contours become entirely lost, and the colors become entirely opaque, something of the palpable breath of life is gone and can rarely be regained. In its place, there is often a heavy, overworked quality.

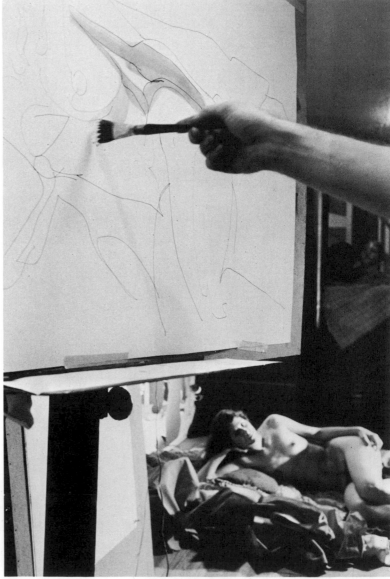

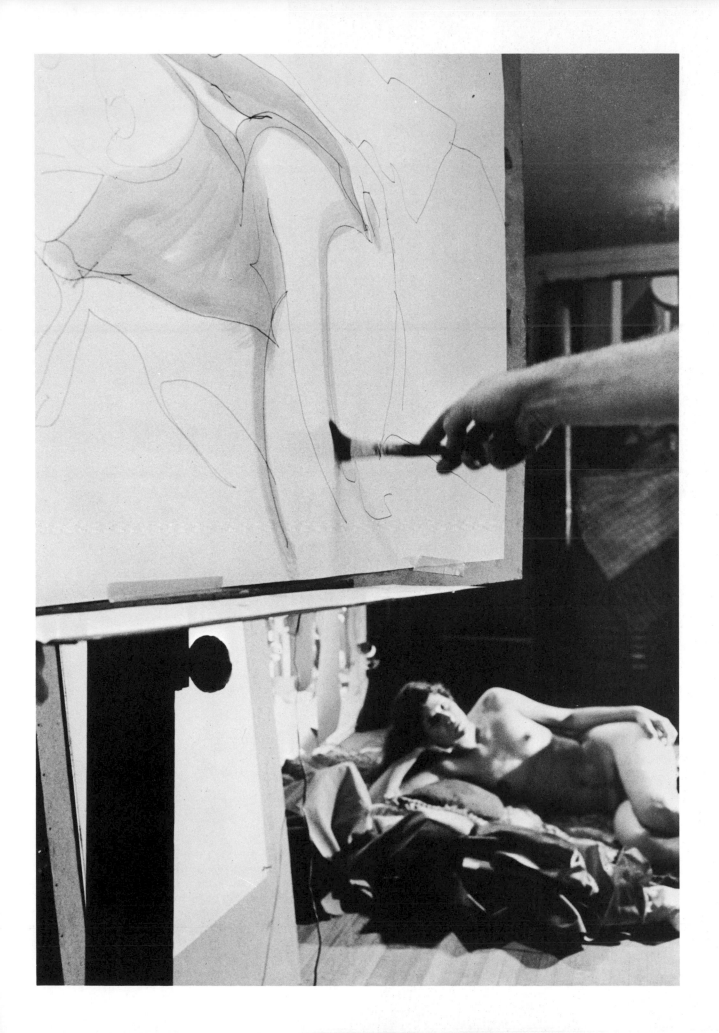

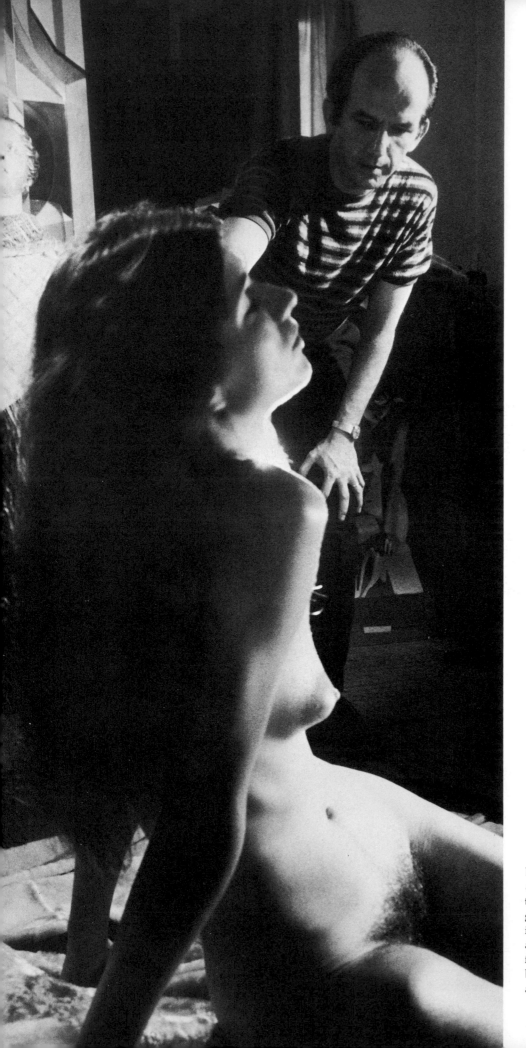

Even at the initial stage of posing the model and arranging the lights, the artist should have the medium he intends to use in mind. If he's going to use acrylics, tempera, or silkscreen in traditional flat-shape relationships, or paint applied with a palette knife, he had best arrange for the various angles of lighting that produce bold slabs of light and shade, such as directly above and to the side at a ninety-degree angle.

For Ingres-like rendering—muted and diffused—cast shadows produce subtle and pearl-like gradations. The pose of the model is especially important in setting the tone. For clarity and rendering of mass, the artist should adopt a vantage point either very low or three-quarters to the side or back, so that the model's actual muscles appear to overlap each other.

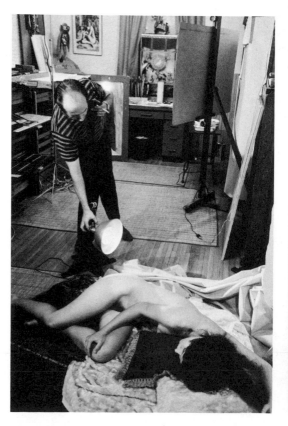

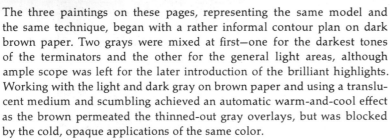

The three paintings on these pages, representing the same model and the same technique, began with a rather informal contour plan on dark brown paper. Two grays were mixed at first—one for the darkest tones of the terminators and the other for the general light areas, although ample scope was left for the later introduction of the brilliant highlights. Working with the light and dark gray on brown paper and using a translucent medium and scumbling achieved an automatic warm-and-cool effect as the brown permeated the thinned-out gray overlays, but was blocked by the cold, opaque applications of the same color.

If this hard and soft quality is misread by the artist, the most bizarre distortions seem to take place. There's a constant need to clean and dry the brush to achieve the softer blendings. At this point a medium dark gray may be introduced to solarize or "awaken" the reflected or half-lights within the shadow areas, and the final electric crackle of the highlights finishes the work. Occasionally this final highlight makes a major form statement, as it does near the knee (see picture at the upper left), where it divides the leg into upper and lower planes.

At this point very careful attention was directed to the hard and soft edges of the shadows, which are mentioned periodically in this text since they are probably the key to achieving effects of light and shadow. For instance, in the picture at the left, the demarcation of light and shade across the breast—beginning at the right where the arm overlaps the breast—comes out from behind the arm as a form shadow, rises sharply as a shadow cast by the arm, descends in a soft curve of a form shadow, again becomes a cast shadow briefly, softens as it rises, and finally becomes an extremely soft form shadow on the left shoulder.

7 | COLOR AND SPECIAL TECHNIQUES (1)

Color is composed of hue, value, and intensity. Of these three "dimensions," hue and value are the most familiar. Light effects are based on value—that is, the lightness or darkness of a color. If we substitute hue (the rainbow name of the color) or intensity (the brightness or dullness of a color) for value gradations, interesting and unexpected things result that are rarely, if ever, seen in nature. For example, against a blue background, the figure may get redder instead of lighter; greener instead of darker in the shadow areas, and so forth. It may also get brighter instead of lighter, producing weird, unearthly effects. *Thus, any value system of lights and darks may serve as a framework for an abstract use of color in its other dimensions,* which would be difficult to imagine as existing in reality.

COMPLEX AERIAL PERSPECTIVE

We discussed simple aerial perspective in Chapter 5 as a technique for mentally changing light in a picture. Complex aerial perspective is similar but it provides more flexibility and also the capacity to handle a naturalistic image in a more recognizable manner. As our foreground color, we may choose any one of the hues in the rainbow or all of them. Choose, for example, red, yellow, and blue. The further away they go, the more they mix with (a) each other, and (b) the infinity color, until they disappear. It is also possible to make the infinity color an equal mixture of the three to begin with. Thus, a tile floor of infinite-color variety may slowly appear to recede in a striking and tangible way if the individual colors intermix with each other and with the infinity color as it progresses down a hallway into, say, a blue shadow. At the end of the hall, most of the tiles will be subtle variations of blue-gray. The artist often violates this formula, because it tends to deposit all the bright colors at the lower edge of the picture. Thus, you will find the technique occasionally employed in a painting on an informal basis wherever needed. Remember that in nature the warm colors (red, orange, and yellow) tend to advance and the cool colors (green, blue, and violet) tend to recede.

SOLARIZATIONS; REFLECTED LIGHTS; AND COLOR ECHOES

The solarization process in photography, to state it simply, is a technique whereby the print or film is exposed to light for a brief period of time during the development stage. The results of this process are a strengthening of the line of demarcation between lights and darks together with some reversal or negative effects and a general lightening of pockets of tone within the shadow areas. This is an interesting point of reference for the painter, particularly in the handling of color.

If the artist wishes to achieve greater luminosity and stronger shape patterning together with increased emphasis on linear rhythms, he should follow this simple maxim: *emphasize the terminators.* It's always darkest just before the dawn and shadows are always darkest just before the light. We can get at this either by darkening the divisions, or by lightening the shadows up to those divisions. Since the negative approach is usually stronger than the positive in painting (leaving a color is stronger than painting one), lightening the shadows is the better way. Try working into a tonal study of the figure by slowly lightening and brightening these shadow areas, adding contrasting colors at times (red into a blue shadow,

Especially with brush and ink or woodblocks you can transform the continuous tone of reality into full-color flat patterning.

for instance) and at other times introducing colors into the shadows of the figure that appear in other areas of the composition. This produces more the sense of light reflections between forms and their environment (naturalistic approach) and color "countermelodies" or "echoes" (design approach).

CHIAROSCURO VERSUS LOCAL COLOR EMPHASIS

Rembrandt is credited with having said that "local color and the effect of strong light are mutually incompatible." The artist must make a choice as to which will be dominant, although they both may exist in some percentage in the same painting. A more precise rule on the subject might read: "The utmost in explicit modeling of forms under strong light and the purest high intensity in flat shapes of local color on these forms cannot exist together because tone modeling produces tints and shades of that local color (admixtures of whites, grays, and blacks in terms of the actual pigments used to render the effect), and such alterations (a) reduce the intensity of the pure color and (b) break up the flat shapes into subdivisions." This revision of Rembrandt's maxim is far less handy for carving on stone, but it focuses more precisely on the problem as it is revealed in his own paintings.

Venerable art historians like Wölfflin have used this dichotomy to divide all painters into two groups: *linear* and *malerische,* or *painterly* (the *linear* meaning outlined shapes as opposed to the grappling with plastic forms and masses). This choice has a lot to do with the artist's mental approach to light. If he chooses the local color emphasis, his light effects will be those of hue and intensity—pure bright colored shapes, with internal value differences kept to a minimum. If he chooses the light and shade emphasis, he will produce (in the extreme) monochromatic compositions with, perhaps, faint overglazes of color.

In practice, the flat-shape local-color painter will see the model as only a part of a total environmental composition and may use only two shapes to paint the whole figure—one for the flesh tone and one for the hair. He will be tempted to use costumes, accessories, or overlapping still-life elements to produce more interest in the shape break-up of the figure. He may also tend to keep the figure small—possibly combining several figures—with an eye to creating design enrichment to make up for the mass and form modeling he has dropped.

The chiaroscuro artist—and Rembrandt was one—will look for all the value differences he can find, breaking up the forms into strong groupings of light colors opposed to rather exaggerated darks, thus establishing two opposing value saturations, instead of hue saturations as in the former approach. In a more atmospheric medium such as oils, it is wise to keep the darks transparent and the lights opaque. To this end, the old masters used a clear, dark golden paste medium called a "megilp" with their shadow colors and "putrido" whites made by mixing one part oil white with one part egg tempera white. This combination has the textural working characteristics of marmalade and plaster.

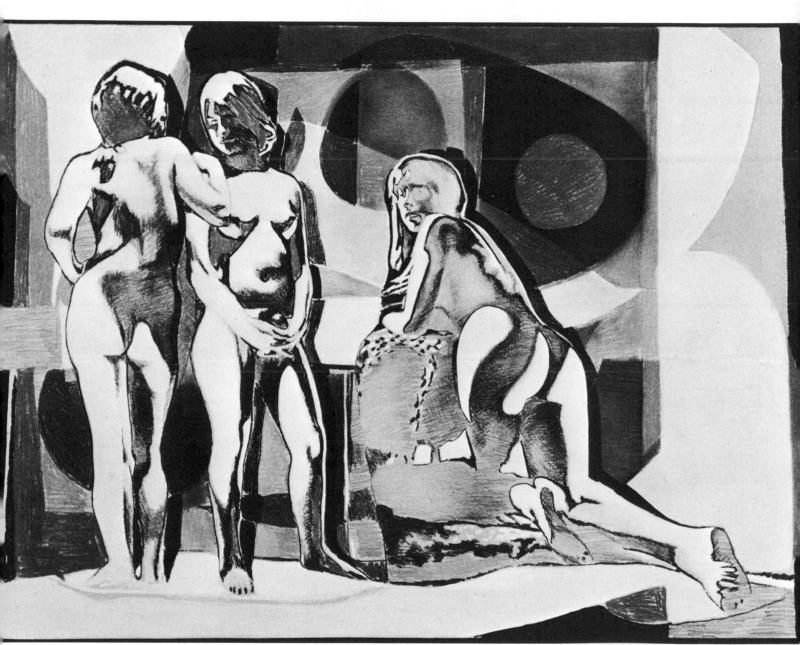

The occasional use of exaggerated solarization creates a tension between the almost ghostly head and shoulders of the kneeling figure and the solidity of the hips and legs and portions of the standing figures. Wherever this effect is utilized, it creates a feeling of a breath of frost rendering what it touches transparent and incorporeal. This is impossible to achieve without preserving most of the original perimeter of the shadow, for once it is lost, the picture dissolves into cloudy indecision. It helps to have some color other than dead white to work into, and pastels on tinted paper, which were used here, are one of many effective media to be used with this technique. Quite often I still find it necessary to add the final touches, especially in the lighter register, with oil or acrylics. Having begun the transformation, I will continue relying heavily on a thick transparent pasty oil medium until all of the pastel has been incorporated into the oil paint. This is done without fixing, since it is almost impossible to fix the pure pastel painting adequately. With enough of a coating to actually hold down the dry pigment, you change the color relationships, especially on a dark tinted ground or if much overlaying of colors has taken place.

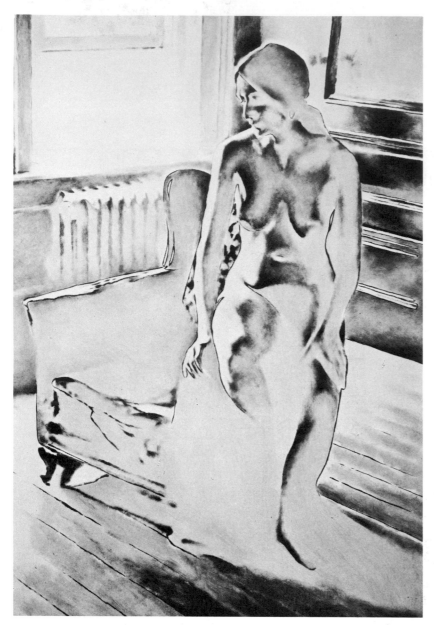

Here the medium was megilp with a faint trace of alizarin crimson and raw sienna, which produced a mahogany tone. The whole effect is conceived of as beginning at a sharp or soft terminator and fading away into a reflected light which is the pure stain of the medium itself—deeper and golden, without any pigment whatever. Large patches like this are left below the knee of the bent leg and inside the arm of the chair. Occasional brush contours were added at the end this time, and only where absolutely necessary, to avoid the feeling of indecision. The reflected lights are so exaggerated that they fall just short of competing with the main lights, and the picture threatens to reverse itself into a negative. Preserving the main light effects in the window, on the floor, and the rim lighting of the chair and the model keeps this from happening, and comprises an approach that seems somehow truer to the two-dimensionality of the painting. The figure is never allowed to become a solid isolated mass, but appears more like a rubbing of a carved bas-relief.

Facing page. This picture can be considered the third in a series of decisions: the first, on page 76, being the general disposition of the basic shape system; and the second, at left above, departing from the relentless hard edge and eating into the dark shapes for half lights. Now, in the third stage, color is "pumped into" the areas within the shadows that have been eaten away. I often call these "canal-lock" reflections since they are like little pools of colored water in between hard or soft barriers—or perhaps the concept might be compared to cloisonné in enameling, where vitreous colors are melted into the spaces in a wire design. Remove the barriers and all is lost.

The three pictures on these pages represent the visual-mixture approach to value as interpreted in three different media, with resulting differences in sharpness and general atmosphere. The painting at left is a greatly reduced pen drawing on absorbent paper. The directional movements of the lines follow the contours of the anatomical masses of the figure in part, and in some areas, especially the lower right waist of the figure, simply flow out into the background, where they begin to ebb and flow as either harmonious or concentric reverberations (such as the background at the upper right shoulder) or confront the contour with direct opposition, as is the tendency down the entire left side of the figure, producing a pronounced effect of space and depth. Through influenced overlays, these impulsive movements of tone are unified by a warp and woof that, unlike the threads in cloth, thin themselves out and disappear entirely in light areas. Often the contours, where they seem important, must be reemphasized to compete with the visual mixture lines. The scratchboard composition on the bottom of the picture below represents a removal technique, and the contour lines here are in reverse except where whites have been eaten out on both sides of a remaining black line. Essentially the same visual-mixture approach with pencil on the facing page results in a more diffused effect relieved by the bolder cast-shadow accents executed at the end.

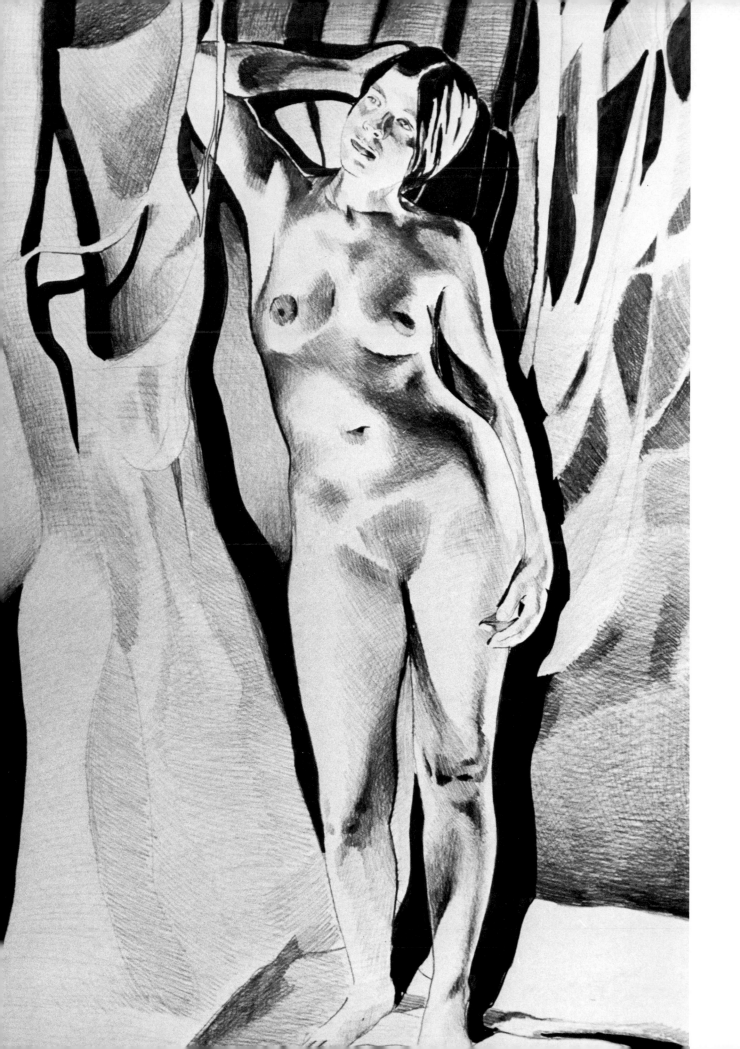

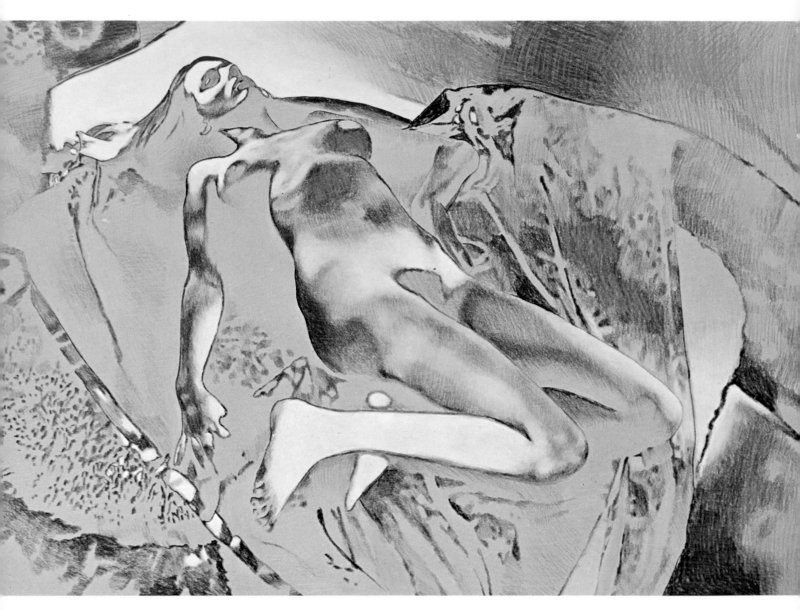

With this picture we approach the extreme limits of the solarized image or intensified reflected lights. The figure is fragmented by the tensions between main and subordinate light sources and creates a lost-and-found effect with the equally strong lights on the drapery. Note the tremendous difference between the intensified chiaroscuro effect in this approach and the local color approach on page 97 in which nothing is done to completely break the silhouette of the figure. Sleek highlights and muted shadows are decisive, but the density range is very shallow considering that there are more than three tones dealt with in the figure. However, in an absolutely pure flat-shape treatment, tonal variations would disappear entirely. When forms are shattered by light effects, as in the painting on this page, there is an atmosphere of turbulence and drama and emotion compared with the placid and decorative logic of the local color approach.

There is far more ambiguity and possibility for transformations and optical illusions when light shapes are treated as entities in themselves, even though they encompass more than one physical element.

The same drama and turbulence can be kept within the boundary of the figure, placing the image halfway between the two just described. It is a silhouette only because there is nothing in its surroundings for these widely disparate elements to hook onto. There is more of an oily or metallic quality to the flashes of light across the breasts and down the arms, which is probably due to the greater fragmentation of small shapes together with the softer edges.

To indicate as much mass and light and shade as possible with a rising and swelling contour line and several carefully chosen shapes can be compared to the art of writing a Haiku poem. The finished work has the appeal of half-finished marble bas-relief. The hand and the feet in this drawing seem to disappear into the uncarved block, creating a mysterious effect and at the same time avoiding the problem of having the figure appear to swoop in one part of the picture and out the other. In the drawing on the facing page, the swelling and contrasting lines do nearly as much as the shadow indications to describe the fluctuation in the elements of the total mass. When the line thins, the forms seem to be swelling, as if trying to burst the boundary. When it swells, it seems as if there were a little sliver shadow between the figure and the background. There is nothing like a sensitive brush to make the figure come to life. It is the final gamble, and the results are all or nothing.

8 | COLOR AND SPECIAL TECHNIQUES (2)

It is possible to emphasize the *reflective, transparent,* and *translucent* effects one sees in nature and, after ascertaining their essence, to use them for purely artistic or design purposes, since these phenomena transform or extend the subject matter in interesting ways.

The main principle of natural reflection is duplication which causes multiple images. If the effect is diffused, we see glowing islands of light and heightened contrast.

The model may be given the dazzling quality of metal or glass if highlight structures along the ridges of muscles are emphasized by trapping them between darker tones adjacent to them which move out into medium-value reflected lights along their perimeters—in other words, light in the middle, then dark, then gray at the edges. The darker the divisions between these highlights and the surrounding local color, the more brittle and metallic the resulting effect. The highlights should not be trapped by a relentless outline, however.

The model may heighten the reflective qualities of her body by rubbing suntan oil on her skin until it is slick and shiny, or the artist may photograph her in the shower, under a spray from a hose, or emerging from a lake, and so on.

Translucencies or transparencies may only be detected when they partially distort or muffle forms seen behind them, as when we look at objects through sheer material or a glass goblet, for example. Imagine two still-life setups—one in which you have an opaque shiny white goblet against a white background and one that is a perfectly transparent goblet against a light background. Unless you would show the back of the goblet through the front of it in the latter case, the renderings would be identical. Now if you slide a piece of graph paper behind each goblet, the difference becomes apparent. In the first instance the opaque goblet blocks the graph paper. In the second, the transparent goblet distorts the markings on the graph paper seen through it. This phenomenon has to do with light and how it is changed as it passes through various materials or is either directly reflected from surfaces or diffused.

The artist can accomplish an interesting variation on some of these natural phenomena, for example, by drawing shapes on top of tone renderings and distorting what is inside this perimeter. He may distort the linear connections, giving the quality of refraction, wavy lines, and bulges as if a lens had been placed on top of the image, or he may produce a new and foreign color saturation here, achieving the quality of simulated transparency.

NEGATIVE REVERSALS

The artist who has at least a nodding acquaintance with photography knows that often the negative shows more promise, more design substance, than the resulting print. He may choose to work from negative reference or to change the colors as he paints from what he sees to the opposite.

An absolute, relentless reversal of all colors or tones is too mechanical for the most part and so the artist will sometimes reverse a few and leave others the way they were.

When reversing colors, we often change their natural relationships—and not always for the better. In order to have some criteria for anticipating what will happen, or to analyze what we have done, it helps to study color reversals in relation to the natural order of values.

To show something that we intuitively know to be true is one of the chief functions of the artist.

NATURAL ORDER OF VALUES
YELLOW (lightest)
ORANGE
RED
GREEN
BLUE
VIOLET (darkest)

When enough white is added to a color low on the chart, it becomes lighter than one normally above it. Conversely, when enough black is added to a color that is high on the chart, it becomes darker than one normally below it. In either case, we have produced a _color reversal of the natural order of values._ You must have two or more colors side by side in a composition that are not in their proper relationship according to the chart in order for them to qualify for this phenomenon.

These are some of the most unique and mystifying effects of all color relationships. Whereas at best they are exotic and otherworldly, at worst they are downright nauseating. Much depends on the proportion of one to the other. Equal proportions, say, of light violet and dark yellow will most certainly be unpleasant, but a small circle of one in a large area of the other might produce a psychedelic effect.

When a composition is going sour in terms of color, it is quite often due to unexpected reversals. If one color is removed or changed, or if the two offending colors are separated by a line—or by another shape—or if the proportions between the two are made unequal, the total color effect will improve.

PRISMATIC FRAGMENTATION AND WARM AND COOL COLOR EXAGGERATION

Realizing that white light is composed of all the colors of the rainbow, the Impressionists and pointillists, among others, chose to break it up into its components, creating works of art that possess a dazzling vibrancy. Long before this, Rembrandt realized the necessity of fragmenting white light into warm and cool stages—the warm colors being red, orange, and yellow; the cool, green, blue, and violet. His was a simpler system than that of the pointillists, but it was sufficient to raise his color effects above the heavy lifeless ones in the paintings of many of his contemporaries. For the most part, his tonal system included: (1) Warm shadows; (2) cool transition tones, halftones, or reflected lights; (3) warm lights; and (4) cool highlights.

In Rembrandt's case, we are speaking of very subtle colors—variations of grays and tertiary browns, not the high intensity palette of the Impressionists.

In closing these two chapters on color, let me point out that the working light in the studio may be as important as the light under which the model poses in affecting the colors that appear on the canvas.

Tungsten bulbs have a yellowish cast and paintings done in the wee hours of the morning under their influence often change radically when viewed under the rather bluish light of the dawn. Natural sunlight is best and the north light changes the least throughout the day. If you use fluorescent bulbs, it is wise to make sure that they are balanced between warm and cool, otherwise the room will have a cold glare.

Unusual effects in painting may puzzle the viewer simply because they are unfamiliar.

Facing page. Often backgrounds produced without reference to the model provide a suitable framework for unexpected and unusual treatments of the figure. In this painting and also the painting on page 96—two excerpts from my "cosmic" series of nudes—the figure seems lost in interterrestrial space, and we can accept transformations much more readily than if she were standing on her lawn or even in a mythological but earthly setting.

In my cosmic series of paintings—an example of which appears on the facing page—I use a process involving marble papers or endpapers. In this process, water in a tray is sprinkled with various oil colors and then the situation is altered by rocking the tray, running a stick or a comb through it to produce swirls and patterns, after which a piece of paper is placed on top in order to take a print of the surface. The unique quality of this process is that the configurations of relatively pure color that deposit themselves almost like veins of ore in earth strata allow you to work with colors that would probably be garish and raw if they were applied with a brush. These random effects often make splendid backgrounds or function as abstracts on their own.

To produce backgrounds of this sort—in which the figure may be integrated—monoprints of various kinds are also suitable. For example, with a rubber brayer, roll printer's ink on a crumpled piece of nonabsorbent material, such as wax paper or aluminum foil, then unfold it and stretch it out flat. Place a piece of absorbent paper on top of this and rub it with a wooden spoon to take a proof of the effect. You can also roll out a patch of ink on a slab of glass, spray it with solvent, then take a proof as before. All these are simplified forms of printmaking.

Some other ways to make monoprints are: Drip paint onto solvent-soaked paper or canvas; burn papers, then dissect them and reassemble them; and paste or glue papers onto a surface, then partially pull them up when semi-dry, and repeat the process several times, leaving torn remnants of various layers behind.

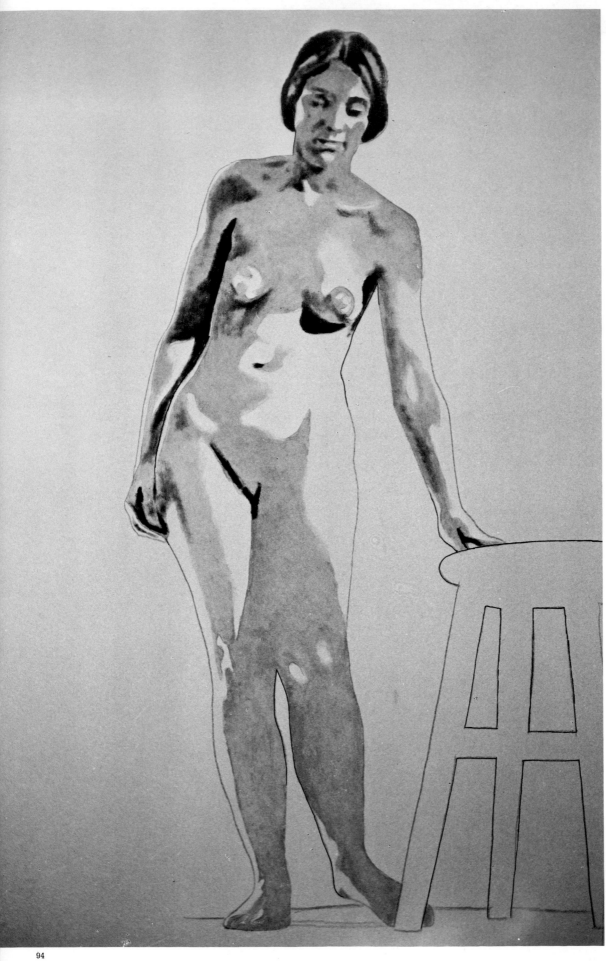

The painting above represents a more conscious attempt at extra dimensional presentiments. The iridescent globe is a symbol of things occult, and the foreground figure appears to be conjuring the other elements through it. The picture wavers between clearly defined fantasy and a fantastic approach to reality, as for example with the arm of the semireclining figure, which emerges into the actual world of the foreground figure, and the arbitrary lines about the head and feet, which add a touch of unreality to the foreground figure.

Transparent or translucent effects in the figure do not always correspond to physical reality. We do not really feel that the figure on the facing page has legs that are made of a less substantial substance than the rest of her body, but rather that we have come upon her as she emerges from nothingness by a decision of the artist. Therefore transitions in relative transparency or opacity can indicate the passage through time or mental dimensions as well as revealing the authentic nature of physical substances.

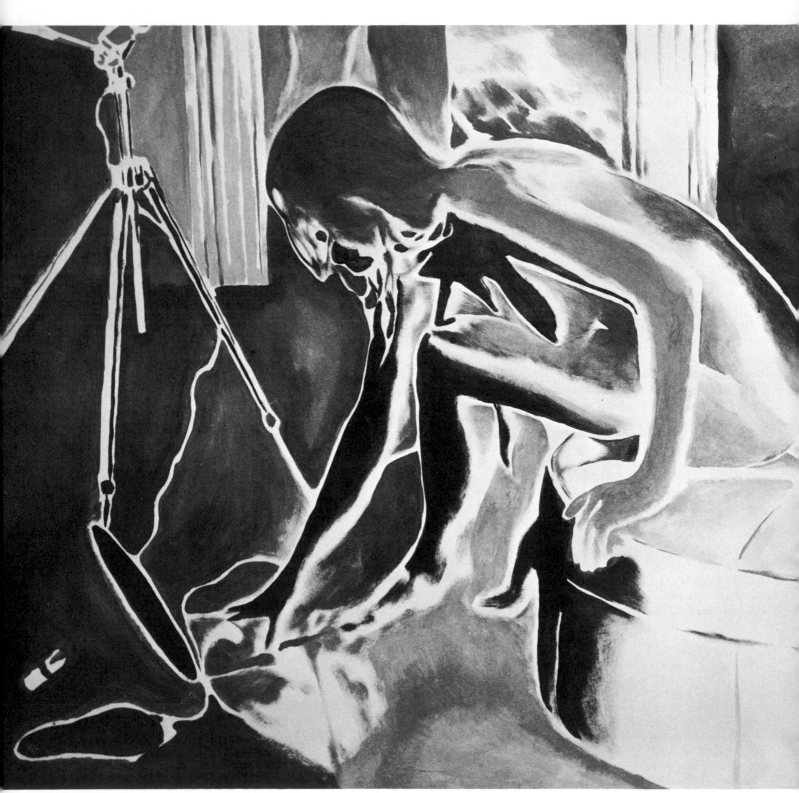

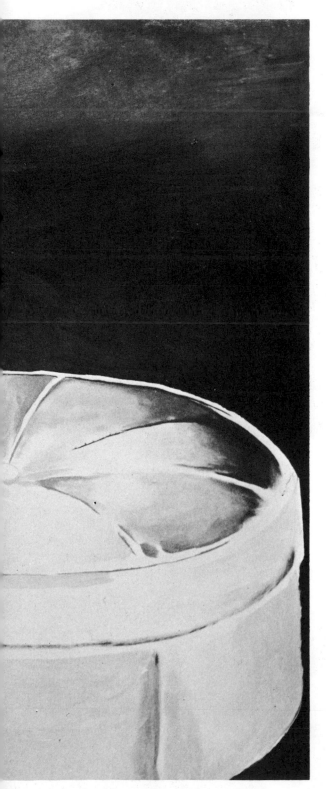

In another example of painting influenced by the solarization concept and once again executed in transparent megilp and scumbling with a mixture of alizarin crimson and raw sienna, the figure is treated in a genre mode, that is to say, realistically, in a scene from everyday life. Thus, the model may be shown as a *model*, in the artist's studio, with easels and other artistic impedimenta about. The backgrounds in genre paintings should be natural and uncontrived, in order to accord with the slice-of-life subject.

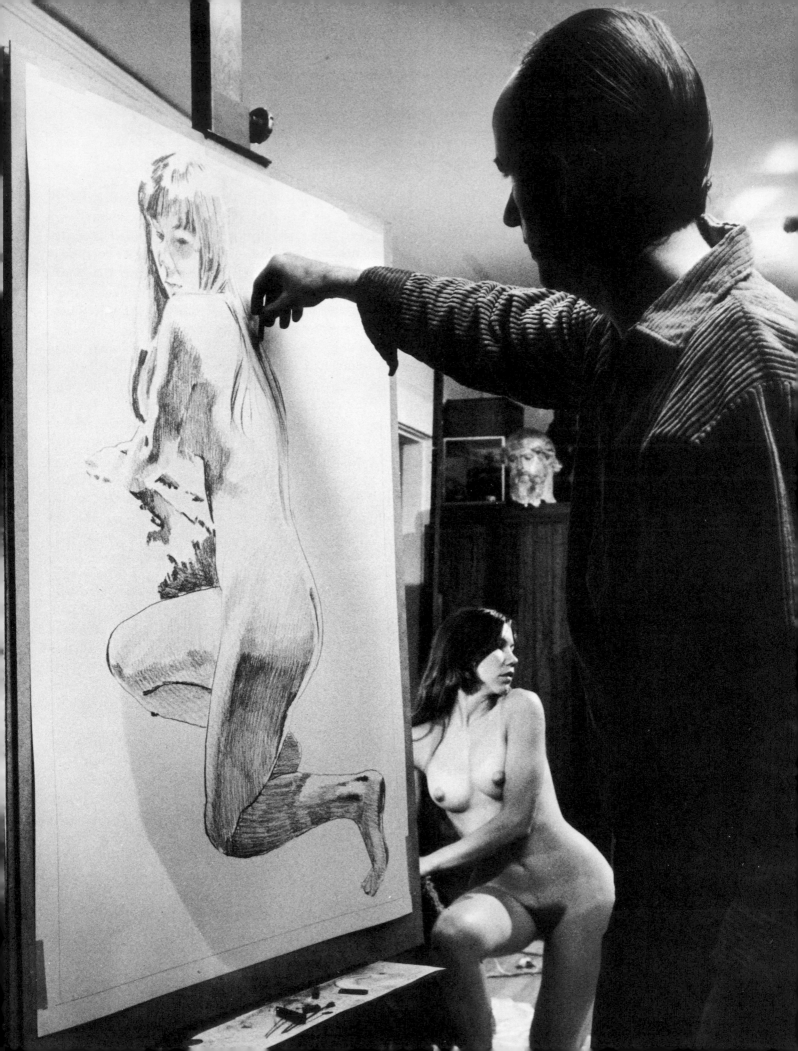

9 | MATERIALS AND TECHNIQUES— LINE AND VISUAL MIXTURES

The scientific side of my interest in art accounts for my fascination with labels, racks, shelves, formulas, scales, and bottles of all sizes and shapes. But a preoccupation with materials and techniques can sometimes lead further away from the artist's primary goal—the production of art through creative enlightenment. Although the following discussion of materials and techniques should have its useful place, no methodology has the power to produce significant art in the absence of insight and inspiration. Indeed, there is often a noticeable decline in spontaneous creativity while the artist absorbs new information. As we might expect, however, he emerges stronger and more capable afterwards.

Pencil, a dry-marker friction medium, is very sensitive to the surface drawn upon. I work a great deal on bond paper, ledger, and "index" paper. The *grade* (hardness or softness of the pencil); the *type* (graphite, Ebony, colored pencil with wax added, and other types, omitting pastel and charcoal for the moment); the *sharpness* or shape of the lead; the *surface* on which it is applied; the *method of application* and the *overlays* (fixative, washes of ink or paint, and others)—these are the variables when working with this medium.

Most pencil-coding systems range from 9H (the hardest) through HB (the median) up to 6B (the softest). For general use, most artists stay within the 2B to 6B range, relying on pressure to change their tones. Previous erasures on paper tend to make the pencil strike dark in that area, so it's best to avoid all erasures until the end if possible, or to rub the paper with the back of your fingernail after a correction until it is smooth, as before. Fixative also changes the nature of paper—even "working fixative," which tends to make the paper shinier and less receptive.

Some artists "sneak up" on their images by starting with hard pencils and gradually using softer ones as they become more sure of what they want. Others, who maintain that at least some of the actual contrasts desired in the final piece should be established toward the beginning as a point of reference for further tone relationships, work alternately with their hard and soft pencils. Strangely enough, the artist is often more committed when he uses a hard pencil than with a soft, because a light mark with a soft pencil is far easier to erase, using, for example, a kneaded eraser, which disturbs the paper only slightly compared to stiffer erasers.

Common graphite pencils are a precise but rather slow and resisting medium to use on a large surface. They generally look too light on, say, a 32" x 48" panel, but after many tone overlays, a pearly translucence is possible. More robust members of the pencil family—colored pencil black and Ebony, among others—are good to introduce at least toward the end of the picture in order to insure impact.

Students may think it's unnecessary to tell them how to sharpen pencils, such as pastel, charcoal, and the rest, but all detailed rendering in any dry-marker medium depends for its effectiveness on hand sharpening of the pencils. The usual method of gripping the pencil and whacking away at it with a knife has all the finesse of killing a chicken. Instead, as shown in the diagram on page 104, you must clear away the wood, then gently whittle down the lead.

With a sharp pencil, you will find that a visual-mixture approach is generally more sensitive than the smudged approach. These visual mixtures are more casual than those

Pastels require a surface with a fair amount of "tooth" to hold the loose particles of pigment.

discussed under pen and ink, but they follow many of the same patterns and movements. Your marks should have direction and a certain incisive quality which may be seen through superimposed tone overlays. When tone smudges are resorted to, the total effect may be lost in a heavy vagueness made even more unpredictable by stray oil spots and old erasures. I am, however, speaking of rendering precision. For impressionistic effects, the cloudy composite of half-realized smudged shapes is often quite effective but almost never concise.

Pen and ink is a most sophisticated medium, since it employs a fine point and depends on the illusion of tone created by textures, patterns, and devices—though in reality it consists of pure black and pure white. Requiring decisive planning and clear directional marks instead of vague blending, it also demands commitment, for ink is usually not erased or painted out with white.

Dark and light are the indispensable components in pen and ink rendering, and the following procedures are basic. For the *darkest* effects in pen and ink, apply as much pressure as possible to the pen point, holding the pen as flat, or parallel to the paper, as possible. (To minimize blotting, always scrape the point of the pen against the jar of ink, then shake it vigorously at a scrap of paper.) Pull your strokes directly back from the point, moving the handle several ways to make this possible.

For the *lightest* pen and ink effects, apply the least amount of pressure to the point, holding the pen as perpendicular to the paper as possible (this will tend to make a scratching sound); pull your strokes from side to side, in direct relation to the direction of the pen point. For the darkest results, you will want your lines heavier, longer, and closer together, whereas for the lightest results, they will be lighter, shorter, and further apart.

The best surfaces for pen and ink visual mixtures are hard, smooth finishes that do not immediately soak up the ink or spread the line, such as index stock, ledger paper, illustration board, poster board, and bristol board.

Most of my comments on pastel are covered by the section on the handling of pencil. I use three types: pastel pencils, hard pastels, and soft pastels, often in that order, since pastel pencils allow the greatest precision, while soft pastels produce the most vivid color. I often find it necessary to add the final touches, especially in the lighter register, with oils or acrylics.

Compressed and vine charcoal are really in the same family as very crumbly dry-markers. All of these media will give lines of unexpected sharpness (in varying degrees, of course), if you begin with a rather fine point and always pull straight back as mentioned earlier.

You may fix all black, gray, or brown pastels or charcoal without too much fear of altering the color schema. Often it is good to fix them first, then rub them down with a pastel tone, and then continue with full color. You have the option of carrying the work into oils or various media if the total effect seems weak and incomplete, as pastels, alas, often do.

Remember that pencil is a medium that is naturally faint, thin, meager, and slow.

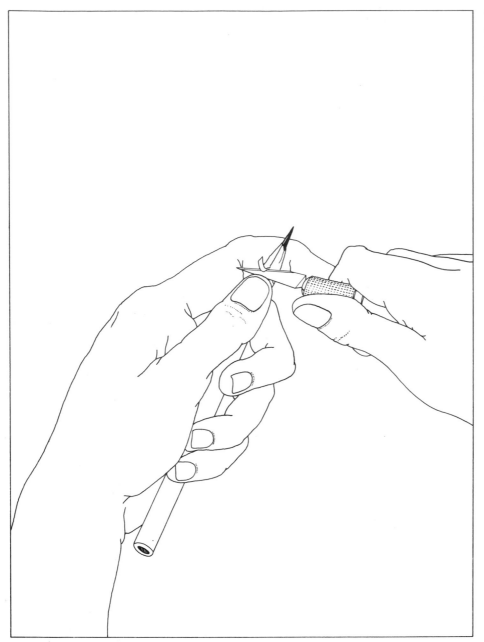

The drawings on the facing page illustrate varying ways of holding a pencil for different effects. At top left, the position in which the pencil is held produces a virtuoso solo line, sensitive and fragile, but not as bold as with other positions. The next illustration shows the position for achieving the subtlest tone overlays and ghost images. At the bottom left, you see a backhand method, in which the pencil moves back and forth along the length of the pencil rather than from side to side. If held relatively flat against the paper, it continually sharpens itself with this method. At bottom right the way to draw the greatest power from the pencil is shown. You grip it firmly, with the index finger directly over the lead.

The diagram above illustrates the best way to sharpen artists' pencils (including charcoal and pastel). Note that the left hand does all the work. When you grip the pencil as shown in the diagram and push the knife blade with the thumb, the thumb actually touches the dull side of the blade. At the same time, the other fingers retract or pull back the pencil. The index finger should be under the soft fragile lead, in order to protect it. No need to worry about cutting the index finger if the thumb of the same hand is pushing the blade. The right hand should only be adjusting the angle of the blade and supporting the weight of the knife. The knife should be razor sharp, since the extra friction of a dull blade is enough to break a 6B lead.

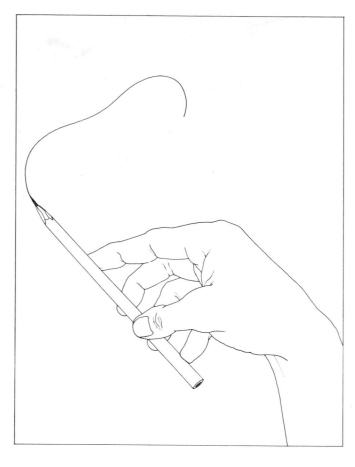

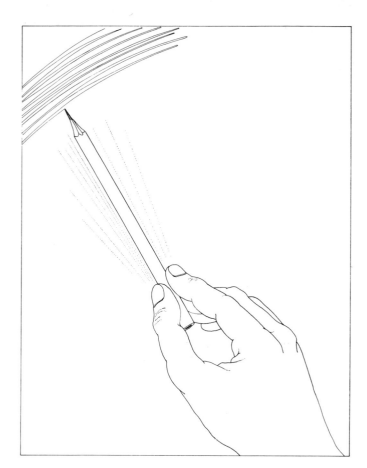

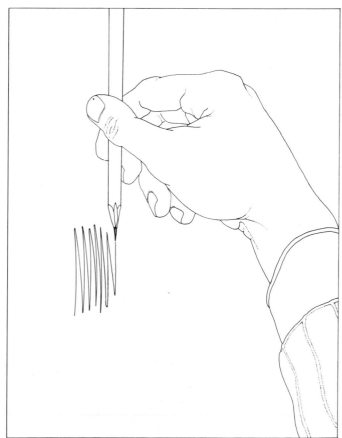

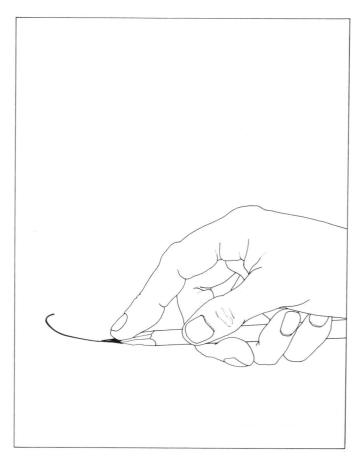

In these three pencil drawings, note the contrast in approach between the slashing attack of much of the drawings at the top of pages 106 and 107 and the relatively quiet craftsmanship of the drawing on the bottom of 106. In the rougher sketches, the pencil was held near the back for the full effect of the side-to-side waving motion, and I choked up on the shank for a darker tone. If you hold the pencil in a backhand grip (as in diagram three on the previous page), relatively flat against the paper, it produces vivid lines. For the very darkest marks, grip the pencil firmly, pressing the index finger directly over the lead as in the last diagram on p. 105. In a full-tone rendering, try marking off a border around your paper so that you won't be afraid to go to the edge of the composition with modulations. Often the peripheral tone accents the central image. Space pockets, produced by the negative approach of surrounding light areas with dark, demand strong peripheral contrasts. Notice how the figure is chiseled out of the surrounding space by the dark around it in the drawing at right and on the facing page.

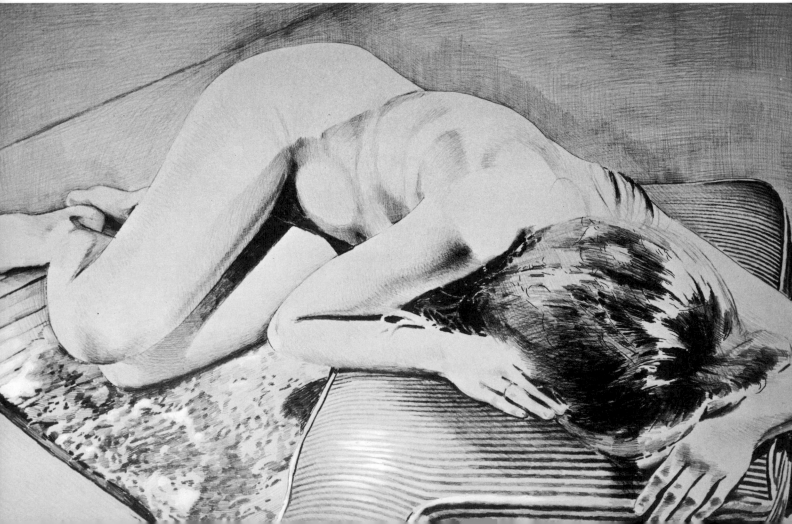

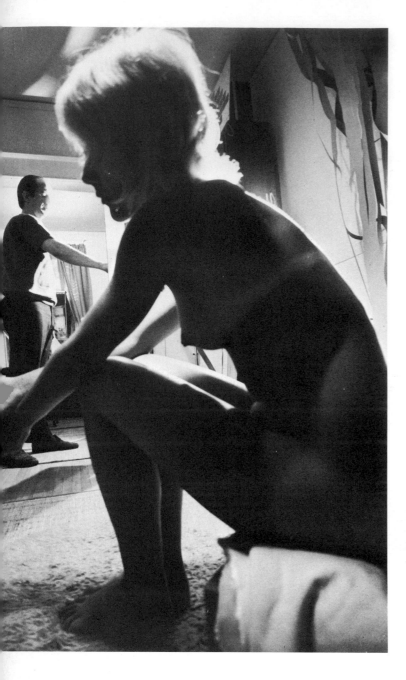

Even with hard pastel sticks—a relatively coarse medium compared with most other dry markers—a classic pen and ink approach may be used on a large scale with spontaneity and flexibility. Once your patterns have been set in motion, they tend to grow and spread and interrelate like parts of an equation, seemingly following their own laws. If you bring them to a blended smooth finish, the clues will be gone, and future development may prove puzzling.

Although it may seem strange, paintings or drawings which end up looking quite finished and realistic are often started in the schematic though bold way shown below, and the "footprints" hidden only at the very end. Depending on the media, very rough and impressionistic beginnings are not always wise, as for example when they require future changes that are not always possible.

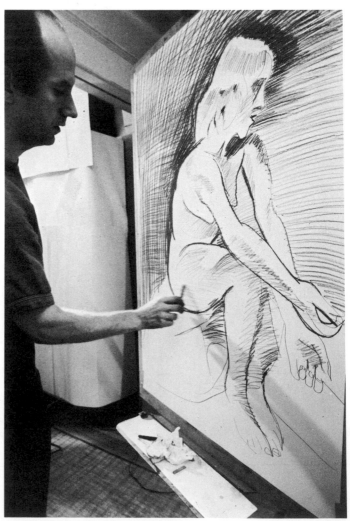

The warning about rough beginnings applies also to media that involve more rigid discipline, such as engraving, scratchboard, transparent watercolor to some extent, and, indeed, any media relying on transparency. If a finished effect is desired in these media, it must be sought from the very beginning. To keep the artist from producing a sterile and lifeless work, it is helpful for him to be able to draw on his experience with more kinetic techniques.

Several directions are available, however, for a picture at the stage of development shown on these pages. It may be left as it is, which may be quite sufficient and better than what would result from further development; it may be "perfected" with further applications of pastel and manual blending— you can smear the pastel with a rag and bring highlights back again with an eraser or light-colored pastels; or it may be developed into an oil or acrylic painting; or, finally, you can simply use it as a reference for a future picture.

Pen-and-ink drawing is often begun with continuous or interrupted contour lines, but when you plan a full-tone rendering, don't simply outline the figure and the light shapes. There are several breaks in the outer edge, and also a great many calculated overlaps where the outer line moves on into the internal parts of the figure, as in the drawing on the facing page, where we see the contour line proceed over the shoulder and directly down the spine, for example. Even more crucial and unpredictable are the shorthand devices used to demarcate divisions between the light and shade and at the same time indicate how and in what direction and with what intensity the tone will roll away from the terminators. Note this especially in the rather informal treatment of the drawing on the lefthand page. The cast shadow rolling out from under the elbow at the waist is indicated with a solid line, moving into a form-shadow division. The directional marks indicate a tonal roll down and around the hips, quite different from the direction taken by the tone under the light patch on the shoulder. The vaguest of initial plans such as the fragile notation of the shoulder blade is still noticeable and susceptible to future development, even though it is somewhat submerged in a tone that partially crosses it. These early notations are gradually lost as the tones are combed through successive overlays as in the drawings on this page.

Facing page. The figure in the pastel painting is treated almost as an ornament, like part of an art nouveau border above a doorway. Nearly every accent in the background is used to frame the silhouette in concentric outward-going ripples. In its original state, the figure had an awkward and unconvincing relationship to the floor plane, and the hint of table and a washbasin; no realistic environment seemed to fit. Then the entire background was painted with a mixture of thin shellac—the main ingredient in traditional fixative—and black pigment which dried to a matte tooth and accepted the final design elements readily.

In the studies on this page, the figures appear to be in various stages of disintegration, especially the one at the top left. They are held together by *connotation* rather than by any formal structure, because some of the light or dark shapes link up more strongly with the background than with other parts of the figure. The entire composition, however, profits from the spreading of interest throughout the entire surface.

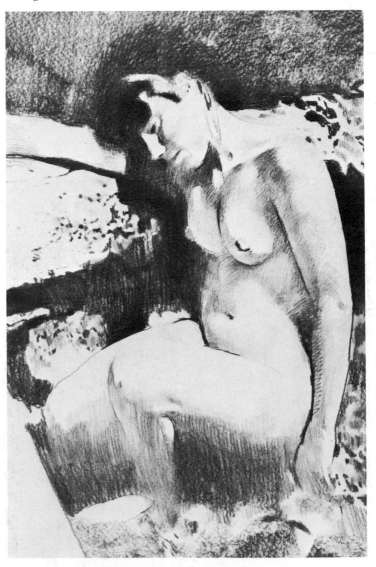

Each medium creates its particular light effects even though it does not necessarily change the actual tonal range or the placement of areas of light and shade. Dry marker media tend to give more surface detail and a surface documentation whereas the heavier liquid media tend to generalize more, creating greater substance and bulk.

With pastels, a scratching or gouging motion is better than aimless scribbling back and forth, which smooths down the surface and makes further application difficult and strained. If this occurs, a light coat of workable fixative, sprayed from a distance, should build up the surface again. After fixing, you could carry the work into full color. Although the brown pastel can be fixed without changing the color schema greatly, a finished full-color pastel is a different matter. It is almost impossible to fix pastels adequately. With enough of a coating to hold down the dry pigment, you change the color relationships, darkening the lighter colors disastrously and lending an acid, garish quality to the mellowness of the high intensity middle value range. The only real solution is to mount pastels under glass.

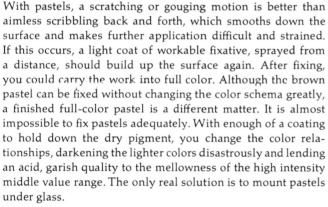

Pastels, like oils and tempera, remain remixable throughout the progress of the work, thus allowing cross-blending of patches of colors and producing great subtleties that rarely happen when colors must be mixed and adjusted beforehand on the palette. (Temperas do dry quickly, but can be reworked with a wet brush.) Therefore, a blue shape may be drawn with the pastel and with that same pastel a red shape elsewhere in the composition may be blended into a red violet. This can be accomplished with a few streaks of blue which are later rubbed in with the finger. While the fingers have red violet on them, this faint stain may be used to alter very subtle light shapes on the figure and elsewhere. In many areas of the picture's background on the facing page, a varied constellation of colors was set down at first, and then another color was worked into each one of these to a greater or lesser extent. Then the shapes were blended manually, resulting in a color saturation throughout. Often you go through this process only to reach again for greater contrast by reversing the approach and emphasizing color differences.

The same general approach as that used with the brush and ink and scratchboard is utilized in planning a linoleum block or wood block. The block can either be executed directly or from a previous sketch.

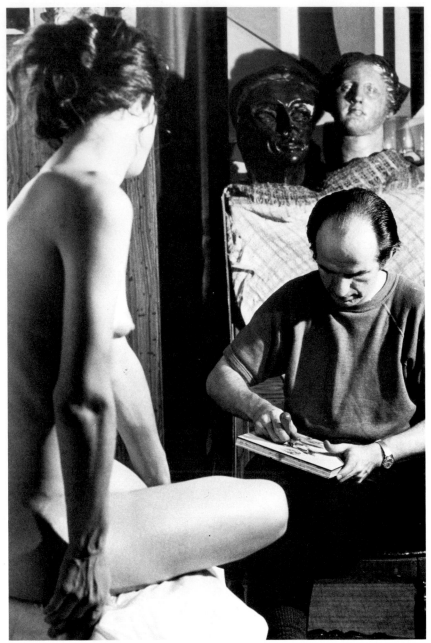

Overleaf. This was an exercise in which I worked neutrals and complementary colors into an extremely intense red violet. The warm tone has almost been entirely suppressed, and yet it seems to permeate the overlays with an underlying glow that is almost impossible to get with direct application. Although parts of the figure were blended to achieve a smooth rolling tone, and also parts of the background, to push them back in aerial perspective, blending the entire composition would assuredly have detracted from the lively effect of the remaining pastel marks.

Type-high blocks are used which can later be printed on a letterpress like the motorized Chandler and Price pictured here. The possibility for producing multiple images in any of the forms of printing or printmaking provides a special excitement all its own. Those who are intrigued by processes or by tools and equipment enjoy the contrast between the emotional appeal of the model, for instance, and the cold metallic power of the machine.

10 | MATERIALS AND TECHNIQUES— WATERBASE PAINT AND OIL PAINT

Waterbase media include acrylics, casein, tempera (under which I classify watercolor), and egg tempera.

Acrylic impastos hold well and do not crack. The coloring power is weak, especially when a light color is placed over a dark—say a yellow over a black—but watered-down layers possess translucency and admit some blending control. A whole palette of dried acrylics may be softened and removed after laying soaked paper towels on it for fifteen minutes. Acrylic gel provides more blending control, but you must know when to stop and let the whole painting dry for a while, because half-dry gel will scar and blister if tormented excessively, and this invariably happens in favorite parts, where you've worked for a long time. Whether scumbling, blending with gel, laying on a thin wash, or any other technique, realize that acrylics reach a certain point where they no longer blend. You must let them lie in peace at this point, or you will rip and scar the coating. In short, acrylics are translucent, rubbery, flexible, and "set" or "liver" when partially dry.

Caseins, when dry, are more rigid, brittle, and solid than acrylics and are more of a danger to a good brush because they will not bloat and come loose in warm water. Always dip your brush in water before using casein (this is a good idea in general with any fast-drying waterbase medium). Caseins are also denser, more opaque, and have more matt finish than acrylics.

Tempera can be described in much the same terms as casein, except that it is a little more brilliant, but will admit almost no impasto without later cracking. It is the leanest of all media and therefore the most brittle, but it is re-miscible, and therefore reusable after it has dried. Since tempera is resoluble, you can go into a dry tempera shape with a damp brush charged with another color and stroke it into the first color until the two are thoroughly blended. Hopping and skipping around a composition with this technique establishes very strong color harmonies.

Egg tempera may be used by itself or as an underpainting for oil painting (this may be said of other waterbase media, too). It may also be used with oil paints and on top of oil paints, but with discretion since you don't want to violate the rule of fat paint over lean paint. By itself, egg tempera permits washes, scumbling, and visual mixture cross-hatching, and at best, blends like oils and dries like tempera. However, you should avoid rough scumbling over half-dry layers, or they will tear through just as acrylics do. Egg tempera also reaches a point where it has "had enough" for a while and must be allowed to dry, but its drying period should be several days. Do not stack egg temperas in a pile, even if they feel dry, for a thick egg tempera painting will take weeks to dry.

Rather than go into detailed descriptions of the chemical composition and pigment characteristics of each of these media, I will simply highlight their most salient qualities in order to share some of the results of my acquaintance with them. However, since I do love formulas, I can't resist including the well-known and indispensable recipe for egg tempera:

Take 1 part egg (yolk with membrane removed, or whole egg, depending on your religion; artists can become violent arguing over this).

Add 1 part oil, varnish or wax medium—such as dammar varnish, or sun thickened

Oil paint is an excellent medium with which to create the illusion of flesh tone.

oil, or saponified wax medium, and the like.

Shake these ingredients in a bottle and then add 1 part water (or more).

To this mixture, add pigment (or temperas). You may leave out fillers, which are used to make commercial paint inexpensive, and no preservative should be added. Keep the mixture in the refrigerator, but if it spoils, do not put a new batch in the old bottle or it will spoil sooner. Egg tempera may be dissolved with either water or turpentine, but only before it has dried.

Oil paint is handled in four main ways: (1) as an opaque medium—thick, short, and full covering, with or without impasto; (2) as transparent stains or turpentine washes; (3) as half-covering translucent coatings; (4) and as rich transparent overglazes with liquid medium or paste megilps.

When you want an opaque medium, you may use oils like a slow-drying waterbase paint. You can premix colors on the palette ("set palette") in great detail and use them hours or days later. Brushes play an important part in the final result when you use oils this way. Bristle brushes leave grooves, flat sables produce more brilliance but sometimes less expression and palette and painting knives add bulk and substance. Zec (a commercial mixture of wax and oxidizer) may be added to produce a "shorter" or thicker impasto, and other driers, such as "Res-N-Gel," cobalt drier, and others have somewhat the same effect. You can also add talc to stiffen the paint. Scumbling is more subtle with oils than with waterbase media, though slower drying means more waiting between superimposed layers.

You can achieve beautiful lean washes by adding turpentine or mineral spirits to the oils and handling them almost like watercolor. Here the ground makes all the difference.

These, of course, are only a few of the thousands of words and thoughts out of many, many more that might be collected on the subject of painting the nude with oils, and I have only briefly indicated some of its delightful mysteries.

Glazes and half-covering coats definitely set oils off from the other media.

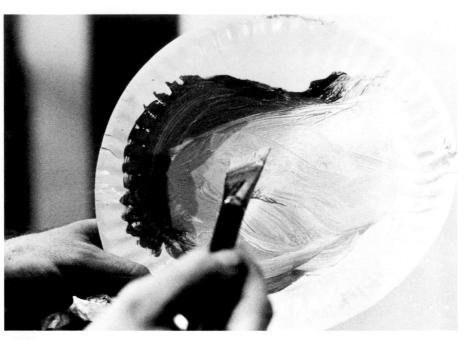

Subtlety usually comes with the longer drying (and longer working) time and the greater diversification of media additives in oil painting. Putrido whites (the half oil white and half egg tempera white) have greater body and retain their strength in diluted glazes. Pure egg tempera whites are also used. The main theory applicable to both is that the lights should be opaque and the darks transparent. Although alizarin crimson, cadmium yellow light, and Prussian blue (ultramarine is more permanent) are the most vivid of the transparent glazes, they are almost always too raw for the subtleties sought in figure painting. More suitable colors might be raw sienna plus permanent green light; alizarin crimson, mauve, and venetian red; alizarin crimson plus raw sienna, and so on.

You can spray turpentine or lean media with a metal atomizer which will help minimize the shininess of these glazes. You can also roll on a paste megilp like Res-N-Gel with a paintroller or brayer to achieve a frosted finish that adds new surface tooth and allows final nuances through scumbling with translucent paints. Colored inks may be added to Aqua-Gel or to egg tempera for another type of luminous glaze, in which case the glaze should usually be over a gray or muted earth-color underpainting.

Overleaf. The indirect techniques in oil media are many. You can, for example, go through all of the previously mentioned steps, starting with thin turpentine stains, then opaque underpainting, half-covering coats, and finishing with oil glazes and final heightening with lights, as was done in this painting.

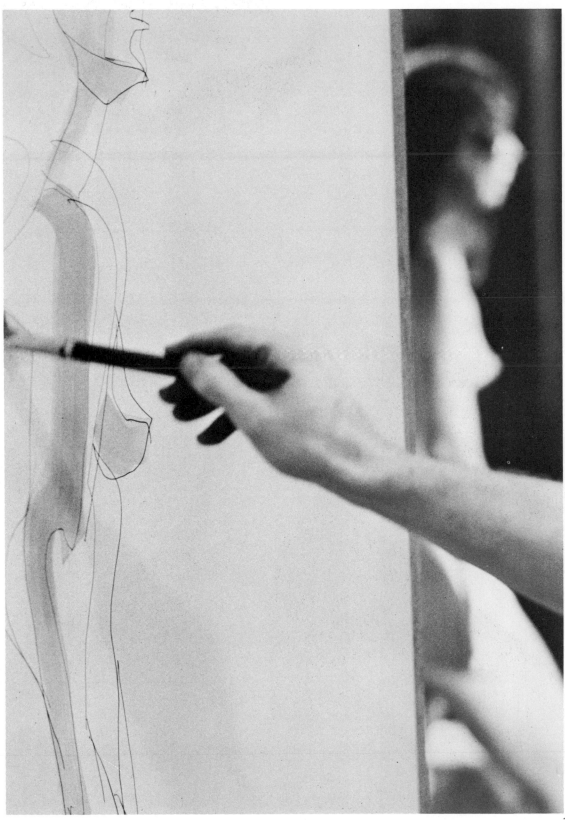

Waterbase whites such as egg temperas are often necessary to give brilliance on top of oil glazes, but these light tones must not be painted in carelessly. Since their edges must be fused with previous contours, it helps to decide which will be the areas of extreme concentration of light and how they are to spread out into subordinate lights and then into transition tones. Any tone should find some pathway, even if only a very small one, to flow out into all the other tones of the figure. The most effective nuances should be applied over a generously but thoroughly dried area of megilp with a scumbling technique. However, putrido whites or egg tempera whites may be applied into wet glazes, too. Acrylic whites should not be used.

Half-covering translucent coatings (usually variations of gray) are most often applied over other painted layers to modify their intensity and effect more total unity. Rembrandt used cool grays to modify the hot earth colors and provide warm-cool contrasts. For example, by painting the figure in hot reds, oranges, yellows, and pinks, then applying half-covering light blue-gray overlays, you can get opalescent tones that you would never achieve with one application.

If the underpainting has a rather full color range, use cool gray half-covering coats over intense underpaintings to prepare for further glazes; otherwise, the colors may become too garish. Heavy, sticky-looking color effects may be made more atmospheric by adding a great deal of talcum powder (colorless when mixed with media) to a megilp and overlaying it.

The waterbase media, such as acrylics, ink, tempera, egg tempera, and so on, allow for a more calligraphic style, especially if you use a sable brush. The marks are more fluid and leave sharper, more decisive edges, and this feature may be used to provide the dominant effect in the painting, as in the acrylic painting on the facing page. Executing a painting in waterbase on an almost nonabsorbent plastic ground, such as in this painting, allows very little controlled or deliberate blending, and there is a danger of cutting through initial tones with overlaying marks.

The spongy surface you get with oil on gesso allows very few sharp divisions, but it encourages subtle variations in tone, especially on the figure, as in the painting below. Egg tempera cast shadows provide a contrast with these oil effects, and there has also been heightening with white on the figure and drapery, so that the oil tones are sandwiched in between waterbase highlights as well as waterbase darks.

Overleaf. We have discussed many of the techniques for handling various materials, but there are still other things the artist should know about liquid media. In considering the ingredients and tendencies of paint, much depends not on the binder but on the manufacturer's proportions and on other factors as well.

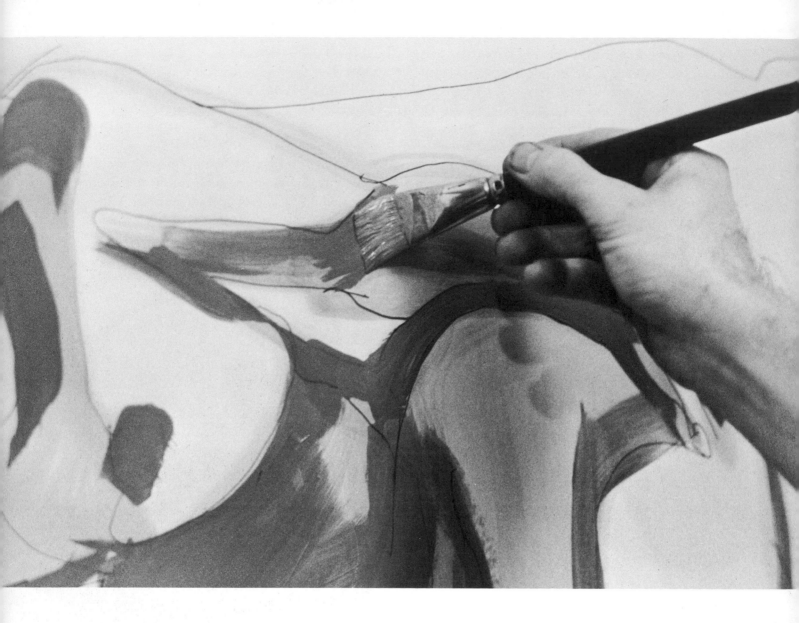

The ratio of the binder to pigment is important. With too little binder, the pigment hasn't enough to hold it on the surface, and may powder off after the paint film dries. *Coloring power* is the ability of a color to affect another or to hide a surface. These are your chief practical considerations in buying paint. With the addition of great amounts of talc as filler (which is inert and becomes translucent when wet), the paint gets less and less opaque and more and more of it is required. As for *permanence,* if fugitive dyes and coal tar derivatives of an impermanent sort are used, there may be temporary brilliance, but the color will not be light fast, and the rays of the sun will bleach it out in time. Some brands of paint are *spectrum balanced,* though the majority (and many of the best brands) are not. Thus, you cannot mix a bright violet by using cadmium red light (an orangish red) and cerulean blue (a greenish blue). You would need alizarin crimson and ultramarine blue. *Consistency* is another consideration, for although it does not always matter, it certainly affects fine craftsmanship to use a paint that has gritty unground pieces of pigment in its mixture. Grinding one's own paint therefore may produce greater brilliance, if the percentage of filler is eliminated, but the consistency may not be as good as otherwise cheaper paint. Try using a glass muller instead of a palette knife—or a mortar and pestle.

While *transparency* may be characteristic of a medium, such as watercolor, megilp oils, stained glass, inks, and so on, it is also a trait of certain colors, generally making them more suitable for glazing. The more transparent colors are alizarin crimson, cadmium yellow light, cadmium yellow medium (and to a much lesser extent, cadmium yellow deep),Thalo green, viridian, Prussian blue, and Thalo blue. White tends to be the most opaque color. Naples yellow and yellow ochre are also quite opaque. As for *miscibility*, colors within the same medium are generally quite intermixable, although colors of different brands may not be. Nowhere is this quite as critical as with acrylics. Monomers and polymers coagulate with each other. For example, Weber and Liquitex will not intermix although it is fine within the same family. *Drying time* is generally a routine matter, depending on the medium. Too long a drying time needed for tempera, for example, would be an indication that there might be too much glycerin in the mixture. These types of abnormalities might be serious, for you do want to be able eventually to trust the paint film.

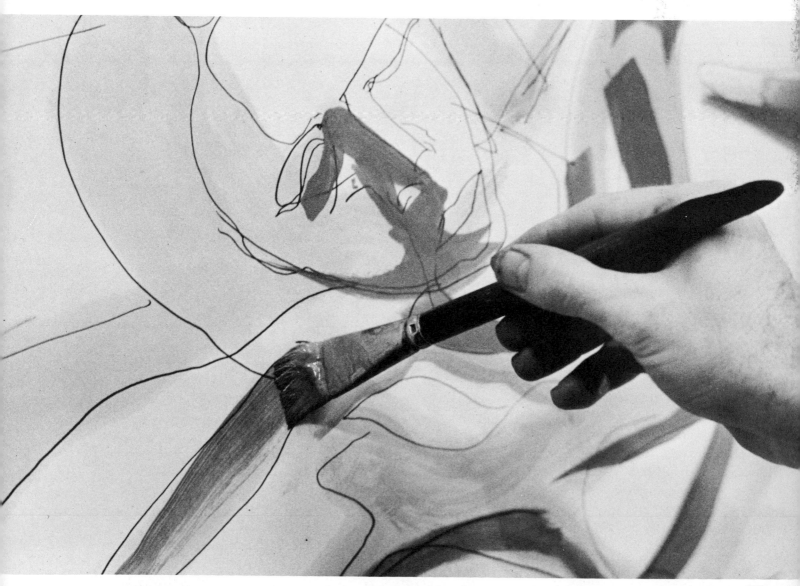

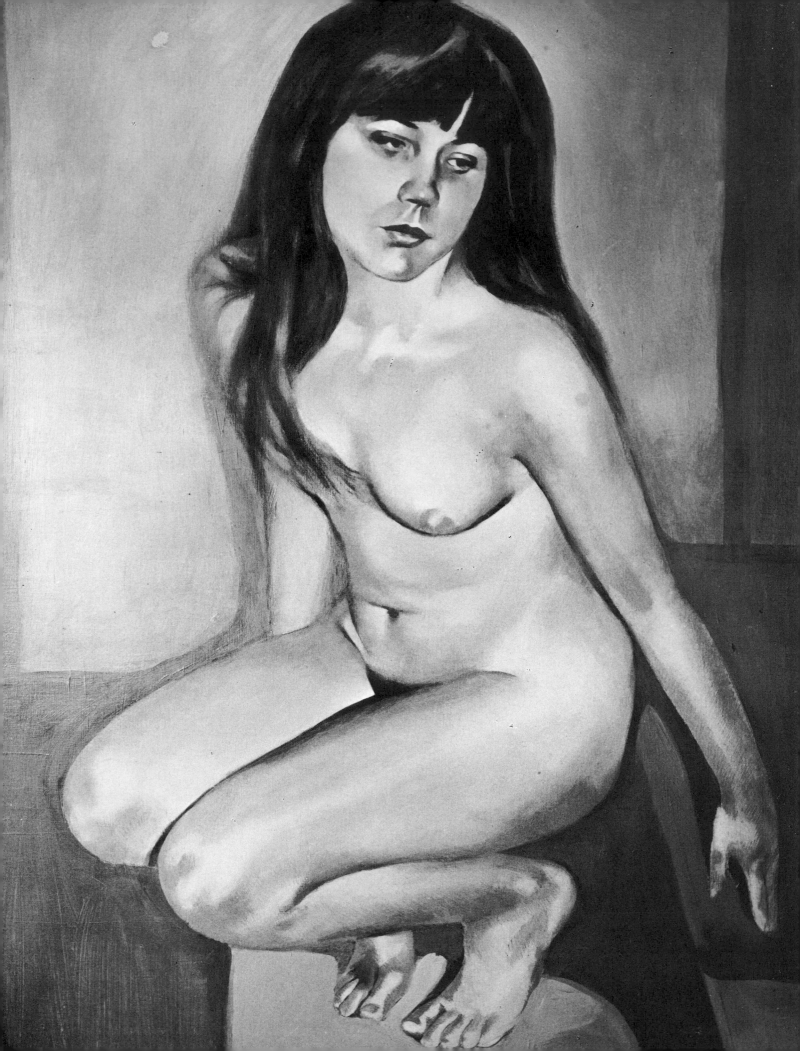

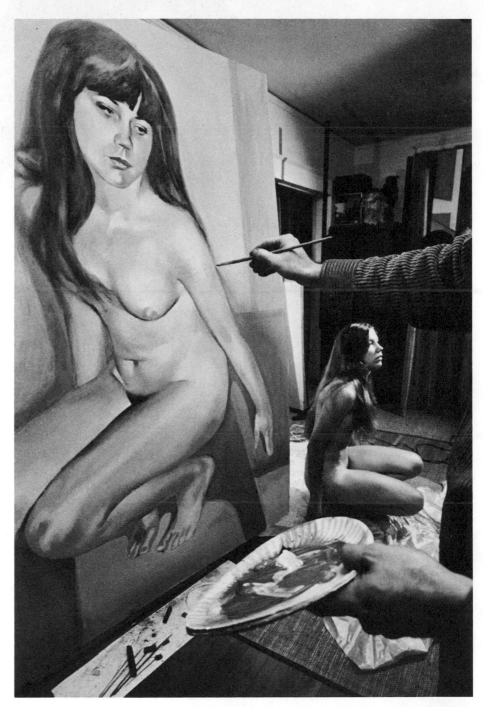

The opposite of involved indirect technique in oil painting is the *alla prima* approach, in which everything is finished at one session, as was done with the painting shown here. If this is the goal, a wet-into-wet technique is best. Simply apply one color to the whole ground—a streaky color is often better than a heavy opaque one—and thin this wet coating with megilp or at least with liquid medium, so that it won't swallow up all of the superimposed colors. The colors of this wet initial ground will influence all of the colors worked into it, insuring some measure of color harmony.

141

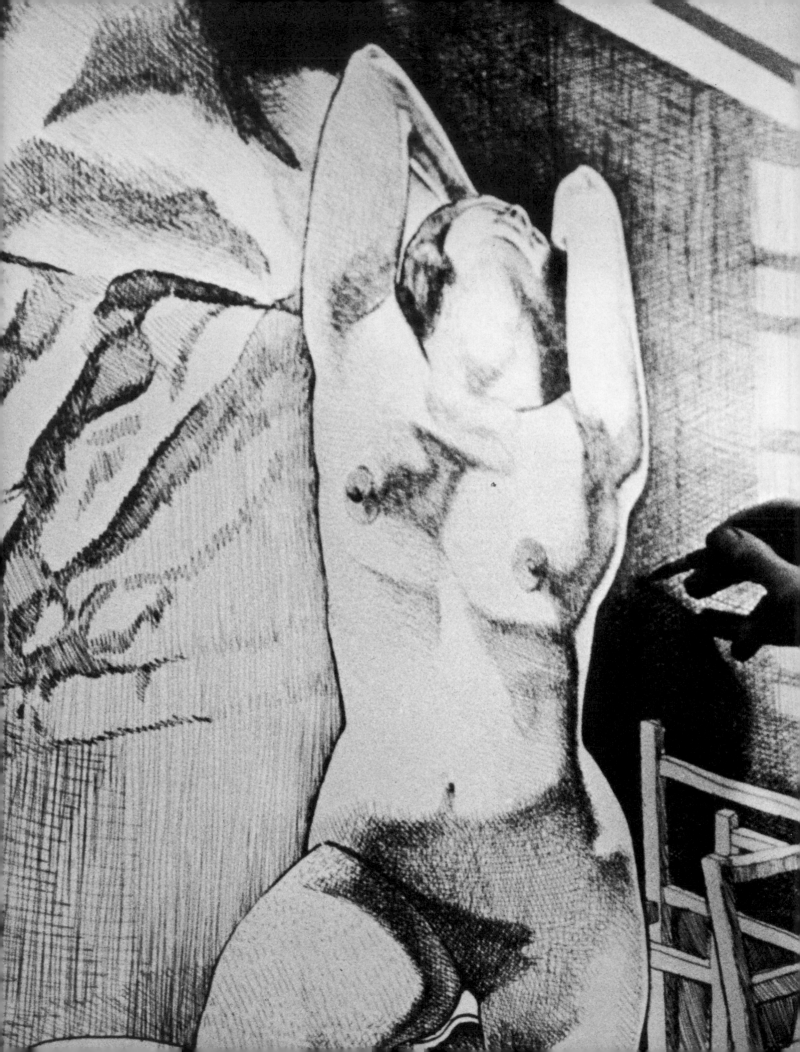

PHOTO CREDITS

Photographs of the artist and models were taken by Burk Uzzle, and the photographs of the art were taken by Ronald Jennings.

LINE DRAWINGS BY ROBIN S. HALL

INDEX